Literacy and Multimodality Across Global Sites

Maureen Kendrick

I0868089

Routledge
Taylor & Francis Group
LONDON AND NEW YORK

First published 2016 by Routledge

2 Park Square, Milton Park, Abingdon, Oxfordshire OX14 4RN
711 Third Avenue, New York, NY 10017

Routledge is an imprint of the Taylor & Francis Group, an informa business

First issued in paperback 2017

Copyright © 2016 Taylor & Francis

The right of Maureen Kendrick to be identified as author of this work has been asserted by her in accordance with sections 77 and 78 of the Copyright, Designs and Patents Act 1988.

All rights reserved. No part of this book may be reprinted or reproduced or utilised in any form or by any electronic, mechanical, or other means, now known or hereafter invented, including photocopying and recording, or in any information storage or retrieval system, without permission in writing from the publishers.

Notice:
Product or corporate names may be trademarks or registered trademarks, and are used only for identification and explanation without intent to infringe.

Library of Congress Cataloguing-in-Publication Data
Names: Kendrick, Maureen, author.
Title: Literacy and multimodality across global sites / by Maureen Kendrick.
Description: New York, NY : Routledge, 2016. | Series: Routledge research in literacy ; 9 | Includes bibliographical references and index.
Identifiers: LCCN 2015043685 | ISBN 9780415859790 | ISBN 9780203713556 (ebk)
Subjects: LCSH: Modality (Linguistics) | Semiotics—Social aspects. | Literacy. | Sociolinguistics
Classification: LCC P99.4.M6 K46 2016 | DDC 302.2/244—dc23
LC record available at http://lccn.loc.gov/2015043685

ISBN: 978-0-415-85979-0 (hbk)
ISBN: 978-0-8153-8194-5 (pbk)

Typeset in Sabon
by Apex CoVantage, LLC

Literacy and Multimodality Across Global Sites

"This book provides a fresh and engaging account of how multimodal methods can be used in a variety of contexts. This provides clear methodological tools with a passion for social justice and the value of literacy in everyday contexts."

—*Kate Pahl, University of Sheffield, UK*

"In this compelling book, Maureen Kendrick offers much-needed international evidence to counteract prevalent home/school mismatch theories in which some children and youth are constructed as under-prepared and their families as lacking. Drawing on her research in East Africa, she resituates literacies in children's varied cultural ways of knowing and expands multimodalities for global geographies and sociopolitical contexts. Through rich ethnographic accounts, *Literacy and Multimodality Across Global Sites* illuminates how people engage and create diverse multimodal forms of literacy in an under-represented area of the world."

—*Karen Wohlwend, Indiana University, United States*

Over the past three decades, our conceptualizations of literacy and what it means to be literate have expanded to include recognition that there is a qualitative difference in how we communicate through modalities such as the visual, audio, spatial, and linguistic and that different modes are combined in complex ways to make meaning. The field of multimodality is concerned with how human beings use different modes of communication to represent or make meaning in the world. Despite the rapid growth of international research in this area, accounts of a broader range of global sites, particularly economically under-resourced and culturally diverse contexts, such as sub-Saharan Africa, remain under-researched and under-represented in the literature. This book contextualizes a range of literacies including health, community, family, and multilingual literacies within broader modes of communication, most specifically play and the visual. The claim is that powerful pedagogies, methodologies, and theories can be constructed by taking a more detailed look at multimodal meaning-making in diverse contexts. By describing and analysing multimodal practices and texts across a diverse range of contexts, the book highlights different constructs, issues, and emerging questions dealing with the study of literacies and multimodality.

Maureen Kendrick is professor in the Department of Language and Literacy Education at the University of British Columbia, Canada.

Routledge Research in Literacy

Edited by David Barton, Lancaster University, UK

1 **Women, Literacy and Development**
Edited by Anna Robinson-Pant

2 **Literacy and Globalization**
Reading and Writing in Times of Social and Cultural Change
Uta Papen

3 **Popular Culture and Representations of Literacy**
Bronwyn T. Williams and Amy A. Zenger

4 **Romani Writing**
Literacy, Literature and Identity Politics
Paola Toninato

5 **New Literacies around the Globe**
Policy and Pedagogy
Edited by Cathy Burnett, Julia Davies, Guy Merchant, and JenniferRowsell

6 **The Discourse of Reading Groups**
Integrating Cognitive and Sociocultural Perspectives
David Peplow, Joan Swann, Paola Trimarco, and Sara Whiteley

7 **Literacy in Practice**
Writing in Private, Public, and Working Lives
Patrick Thomas & Pamela Takayoshi

8 **Children's Literacy Practices Beyond Harry Potter**
Jane Sunderland, Steven Dempster, and Joanne Thistlethwaite

9 **Literacy and Multimodality Across Global Sites**
Maureen Kendrick

Contents

Figures

Foreword

If I had to describe the method of *Literacy and Multimodality Across Global Sites* in one phrase, it would have to be something like "looking back and looking over as an approach to looking ahead." Indeed, Maureen Kendrick does in this book something that is rare in social science research. She takes a bold step back and, with a reflexive gaze, works anew with what she already has at hand. This is not done in a way that simply pulls together a collection of her writing into one book, although in a world of online publishing, such a book would be refreshing, especially in Maureen Kendrick's case and in the context of her richly textured descriptions and compelling visual evidence of children's meaning-making. Nor does it offer new introductions or a "behind the scenes" for her already existing work, although again such an approach could be very valuable. Donald Graves produced a collection of his own writings produced over several decades ago that gave new life to his writing about writing. Sometimes we don't see the full significance of our work when it is first being formulated.

But rather than offer either of these approaches, Kendrick has embarked upon a reflexive journey that seeks to "revisit," as the sociologist Michael Burawoy (2003) might term it, data from various studies across almost two decades of work. As he observes: "The revisit demands that we be self-conscious and deliberate about the theories we employ and that we capitalize on the effects of our interventions" (p. 647). Broadly speaking Kendrick has revisited various research projects in a variety of research sites, ranging from thick ethnographies with one child and her family in a western Canadian city to work with girls and young women as journalists in Kenya. In so doing she has reinterpreted the work in the context of the emergence of new studies and new theories, particularly in the area of multimodality. This is understandable, as she highlights in the opening pages of the book: "At the time that I began researching play, literacy and the visual as communicative practices, multimodality as a field of study was still new, and the limited work that was being done was situated in Western contexts, and based on Western understandings of how modes, particularly the visual, work" (p. 2, this volume). In rich ways she has, in a sense, sought to *decolonize* studies with children and young people from Uganda and Kenya by situating the work alongside other contemporary studies of literacy. As part of this she offers a global perspective, building on her international work in Uganda and Kenya along with Canada and in a university setting at the University of British Columbia that provides an international milieu for study and research. I know from my own experiences in working in settings in sub-Saharan Africa and Canada that this is not always easy (or even welcomed). Sometimes there is critique that dismisses an approach that seeks to find learnings across different cultural contexts, especially involving the Global North and the Global South—and often from researchers in both the Global North and the Global South. Indeed, academic audiences at conferences (especially in the Global North) have been known to act like spectators, prepared to bring shock, tears, and a type of exoticizing surprise to data from the Global South, despite the best intentions of the researcher or presenter to offer an academic and non-sensationalist reading of the data (see also MacEntee, 2015). Kendrick actively resists this, and so we have chapters in which she looks at "sites of viewing," for example, across ages and locations, with documentary photography work with 12-year-old Carl, a student in western Canada' "scribble" drawings from a young child, Nolan, also in western Canada; and drawings for a human immunodeficiency virus (HIV) and acquired immune deficiency syndrome (AIDS) billboard from Rosalee, a school girl in Uganda.

What is also apparent in the looking back and looking ahead is the idea of introducing the work of theorists who might have been around at the time that the research was conducted originally but whose spheres of influence were somewhere else. Working with various theorists in visual studies such as Rolande Barthes and especially applying his idea of "advenience" as explored in 1980 in relation to reflexivity offers a fresh reading and a different angle on multimodal texts. This is the life of the interdisciplinary researcher of the 21st century. We discover that someone else—outside our home base—has produced the perfect lens to look at something that may well have been hidden from view. The data in this way gets a new life, but more importantly our understanding of the phenomenon is deepened.

But there is an additional benefit from this looking back and looking ahead that Kendrick herself inadvertently perhaps, introduces, and that is the idea of the cumulative cultural text of writing about childhood and literacy. Interestingly Kendrick applies this term that Sandra Weber and I first used in *That's Funny, You Don't Look Like a Teacher* to her analysis of some of the drawings produced by children, but I think it is also a fitting term to apply to a body of research over a period of time by one researcher or a researcher team. Weber and I coined the term to talk about teachers in popular culture and the ways in which certain motifs of teaching continue and even become cross-referenced and intertextual in nature. In Kendrick's case, we see her commitment and dedication to the idea of children as meaning-makers through their play and through their use of drawings, but we see in her revisiting practices that the work deepens, and in a sense, it builds on itself. Again, returning to the Barthes's idea of advenience and what could be framed as revisiting, there is the added consciousness of the researcher over time and in relation, for example, to the gendering of HIV and AIDS, sexual violence, and child-headed households (CHHs) that contributes to this cumulative cultural text. As she writes of her own interpretations and rereadings of visual data on "sugar daddies" and risk of HIV, "From a reflexivity perspective, it is my own positioning as a woman that locates my interpretation of this message in a particular way; as a woman I am more invested in the perspectives of women and girls and the issues they face" (p. 123, this volume). It is a recognition of this feminist consciousness that is key. In my doctoral supervision practices, I often say to a student who is passionate about a particular researcher's article or chapter that has been written a few years ago, "Well, what are they writing now?" This should not be taken as a presentism orientation on my part but rather a recognition of the fluidity of our work and its cumulative quality. I might be tempted to cringe at something I published in the past, but then I try also to remember where the ideas came from and how they are evolving.

Kendrick clearly makes a case for the study of multimodalities and literacies in global contexts. There is probably no area of literacy research that is more expansive and promising than in the realm of multiliteracies and multimodalities for talking about the complexities of meaning-making. However, it is work that is sometimes criticized for being obscure in terms of language. *Literacy and Multimodality Across Global Sites* as an accessible text does not seek to simplify and, indeed, by taking on global sites, seeks to add to the complexity.

Claudia Mitchell, PhD
James McGill, Professor
McGill University
Canada

REFERENCES

Barthes, R. (1980). *Camera lucida: Reflections on photography*. New York: Hill and Wang.

Burawoy, M. (2003). Revisits: An outline of a theory of reflexive ethnography. *American Sociological Review, 68*(5), 645–679.

Kendrick, M. (2003). Converging worlds: Play, literacy, and culture in early childhood. Bern, Switzerland/New York: Peter Lang.

MacEntee, K. (2015, March). Exploring the role of positionality in exhibiting participants' visual media. Paper presented at the Comparative International Education Society (CIES) Annual Conference, Washington, DC.

Weber, S., & Mitchell, C. (1995). *That's funny you don't look like a teacher: Interrogating images of identity in popular culture*. London: Falmer Press.

Acknowledgements

PERSONAL ACKNOWLEDGEMENTS

Given that this book has developed over a number of years, many people have played roles in bringing it to completion. Most importantly, I want to thank the many research participants across a wide range of projects in Canada, Kenya, and Uganda. I hope that I have represented their lives, perspectives, and experiences in a way that honours who they are and how they see the world.

A number of collaborators and co-investigators have contributed to the research projects included in this book. I offer heartfelt thanks to all of my brilliant and supportive colleagues at the University of British Columbia, most especially my dear friends and research partners Bonny Norton and Margaret Early. Thank you to my colleagues and friends, Kelleen Toohey and Diane Dagenais, for many influential conversations. My gratitude also goes to my collaborator Roberta McKay.

And finally, much gratitude goes to my husband Michael and my son Nolan for their patience, for the gift of time, for being there, and for teaching me what really matters.

PROJECT ACKNOWLEDGEMENTS

A number of funded research projects have been included in this book. The research reported in *Converging Worlds: Play, Literacy, and Culture in Early Childhood* was funded by a Canadian Social Sciences and Humanities Research Council fellowship. "Drawing: A Window on Children's Literacy Conceptualizations" was funded by a University of British Columbia's Humanities and Social Sciences Research Grant, and Maureen Kendrick was the principal investigator. The project "Literacy, Health, and Development: A Ugandan Case Study" was funded by the Hampton Research Grant Fund at the University of British Columbia. Principal investigators were Maureen Kendrick and Bonny Norton. The goal of this project was to investigate the relationship between literacy and health in development contexts, particularly in relation to the role of women and girls. I offer my thanks to colleagues at UPLIFT-Uganda for their kindness and collaboration, particularly Hizzaya Hissani, Vinita Gilbert, and Tom Gossen. "Digital Literacy and Teacher Development in East Africa" was also funded by the Hampton Research Grant Fund at the University of British Columbia, and Bonny Norton and Maureen Kendrick were the lead investigators. "Systems and Networks of Knowledge Communication in Child-Headed Households in Uganda" was funded through a University of British Columbia Humanities and Social Sciences Grant awarded to Maureen Kendrick and Doris Kakuru (Makerere University, Uganda). This project documented systems and networks of knowledge communication in CHHs (children under 18 living on their own). My thanks to Deborah Namisango Mwebe for her research assistance with this project. A follow-up project, "Supporting the Learning of Children Living in Child-Headed Households in Uganda," funded through a University of British Columbia Humanities and Social Sciences Seed Grant, was conducted by Maureen Kendrick. My thanks goes to Elizabeth Namazzi, who provided research assistance. Our interest was in teachers' perceptions of children living in CHHs and how they address the unique learning needs of these children. "The Literacy Ecology of Three African Communities: Implications for Development" was a Canadian Social Sciences and Humanities Research Council project with Bonny Norton and Maureen Kendrick as the primary investigators. "Using Visual Methodologies" was funded through a University of British Columbia's Faculty of Education Graduate Student Mentorship Grant with Maureen Kendrick providing mentorship to Harriet Mutonyi in the use of visual methods in literacy and health literacy studies in Canada and Uganda. "Literacy, Multimodality and Imagined Communities: Connecting English Language Learners Through Global Learning Networks," a Canadian Social Sciences and Humanities Research Council project, was conducted by Maureen Kendrick, Bonny Norton, and Margaret Early. This study focused on how secondary school students in diverse areas of the world can participate in global learning networks (a learning exchange over long distances) by drawing on and adapting their local multimodal resources for literacy learning. Special thanks to Walter Chemjor for his collaboration on the Kenyan research site for this project. A number of doctoral students contributed to these projects in big and small ways, including Doris Abiria, Ava Becker, Sam Andema, Shelley Jones, Harriet Mutonyi, Elizabeth Namazzi, Lauryn Oates, and Juliet Tembe. Huge thanks also go to Peter Bowra for his ongoing technical assistance with the images for these projects.

Some of the data examples in this book have been published elsewhere. Chapter 1 includes an example of learning through play that was originally published in *Converging Worlds: Play, Literacy, and Culture in Early Childhood* (Kendrick, 2003). Chapter 2 includes four examples. The first was published in *Converging Worlds* (Kendrick, 2003); the second appeared in an article in *Research in the Teaching of English*, *47*(4), 391–419, 2013, co-authored with Margaret Early and Walter Chemjor; the third example was first published in *Childhood: An International Journal, 19*(3), 397–413, 2012, co-authored with Doris Kakuru; the fourth was published in Diaspora, Indigenous, and Minority Education, 1(4), 265–283, co-authored with Harriet Mutonyi. An earlier version of Chapter 3 was originally published in the *Journal of Early Childhood Literacy*, *4*(1), 109–128, co-authored with Roberta McKay. Chapter 4 is an extended version of a chapter first published in J. Rowsell and K. Pahl, *The Routledge Handbook of Literacy Studies* (pp. 619–633). New York, NY: Routledge. Chapter 5 includes four examples, two of which have appeared elsewhere. The first was published in Language & Literacy, 5(1), 1–17, co-authored with Roberta McKay; the second was published in Susan Elliot-Johns and Daniel Jarvis (Eds.), *Perspectives on Transitions in Schooling and Instructional Practice* (pp. 320–346). Toronto, ON: University of Toronto Press.

Introduction

STARTING POINTS

Many years ago, I saw the film *Salaam Bombay* (1988); the protagonist is 11-year old Krishna, who is sent by his mother to earn money in a travelling circus but soon ends up struggling to survive in the streets of one of Bombay's (Mumbai's) poorest neighbourhoods. While trying to earn money delivering tea to people living in a local tenement building, Krishna befriends a drug dealer/ addict and a 16-year old girl whose virginity is being sold to the highest bidder. A subplot of the film involves the relationship between Baba, another drug dealer, and his wife, Rekha, who works in the sex trade. It was their young daughter, Manju, and the play world she creates for herself amidst the chaos and cruelty of the streets that captured my attention. She spends her days playing house, unapologetically and matter-of-factly taking on the identity of a sex trade worker and interacting with characters she creates from her everyday life. There is a raw authenticity in how Manju depicts her life that challenged my conceptions of play and its role in culture. (Interestingly, the screenplay emerged out of interviews the filmmakers conducted with Mumbai's street children about their lives and experiences. Many of these children appeared in the film.) The small scene that offers a glimpse of Manju's play world is something that piqued my curiosity as an emerging researcher and created a desire to better understand the relationship between play and culture, which took me to Kenya as a master's student in the mid-1990s.

When I undertook doctoral studies soon after, I was influenced strongly by the work of Shirley Brice Heath and Brian Street, and I focused my dissertation research on how play might provide another lens for understanding children's situated constructions of literacy. As a doctoral student, I was also invited to join a project with Roberta McKay that posed the question "Do children have images of literacy?" This simple yet complex question was intriguing, particularly because as a new literacy researcher, I was predominantly familiar with linguistic modes of data collection and representation. These foundational experiences with play and the visual mark the starting points of a research trajectory broadly framed within the fields of literacy and multimodality. My programme of research has addressed questions related to how modes other than language provide an opportunity for individuals to tell "stories" about their own lives as traces of layered perspectives, experiences, and ways of knowing.

My interest in writing this book revolves around demonstrating what different modes can show us as researchers and educators about the human condition, spotlighting how we might proceed in a way that changes those conditions for the better. I include a collection of studies that I have conducted over the past two decades focusing on literacies and multimodality in the every day. These studies entail multimodal practices and text production (e.g., combinations of the visual, linguistic, and performative or play-based) in Uganda, Kenya, and Canada. I include a range of contexts across homes, communities, and classrooms and diverse participants in terms of age, gender, linguistic background, ethnicity, social class, and geographic location that add under-represented voices, lives, and experiences to current research and theorizing on literacies and multimodality. The examples are comprised of various ethnographic descriptions that are contextualized in terms of individuals, families, and communities that previously have been neglected in the research literature on literacies and multimodality. Overall, I look at the potential of various modes to create new avenues for individuals in diverse communities to access additional opportunities that allow them to reposition themselves in their sociocultural contexts and to re/imagine their futures. I also forward alternative research methodologies, based on considering multimodality methodologically, as a toolkit for literacy researchers and educators.

CONCEPTUAL, METHODOLOGICAL, AND ETHICAL CONSIDERATIONS

At the time that I began researching play, literacy, and the visual as communicative practices, multimodality as a field of study was still new, and the limited work that was being done was situated in Western contexts and based on Western understandings of how modes, particularly the visual, work (see, e.g., Baldry & Thibault, 2006; Kress & van Leeuwen, 1996). "Multimodality" has become a fresh term for describing how we make meaning in the world using all of our senses (visual, auditory, kinesthetic, etc.). It is an interweaving of cultural, social, cognitive, and biological processes: in many ways, an integration of mind, body, and society (Gee, 1996). All meaning-making occurs through a variety of communicative channels "in which written–linguistic modes of meaning are part and parcel of visual, audio, and spatial patterns of meaning" (Cope & Kalantzis, 2000, p. 5). In general, multimodality is an approach to learning that takes seriously and attends to "a whole range of modes involved in representation and communication" (Kress & Jewitt, 2003, p. 1), whereby modes are considered an organized set of resources for meaning-making (image, gaze, gesture, movement, music, speech, and sound effect), a way of expressing or carrying the meanings of material affordance shaped by generations of the work of people in their social lives (Kress & Jewitt, 2003).

The theoretical domain of multimodality is still an emerging field (Jewitt, Kress, Ogborn, & Tsatsarelis, 2001; Kress & van Leeuwen, 2001; van Leeuwen, 2011) and as such, "there is no orthodoxy" (Jewitt & Kress, 2003, p. 4). Examining the emergence of this new area of research from a multifaceted and international perspective is therefore critical. Yet, despite the rapid growth of international research in the area, accounts of a broader range of global sites, particularly economically under-resourced and politically diverse contexts such as sub-Saharan Africa, remain under-researched and under-represented in the literature. As van Leeuwen stresses in the final chapter of the *Handbook of Applied Linguistics* (2011), because multimodality is a relatively new field of study, there is "much room for further development." He identifies three important areas for the future of multimodality, one of which is "the need for attending to cultural diversity" (2011, p. 679). He argues that

> to date multimodality has predominantly looked at 'Western' modes and 'Western' ways of using them. But just as linguistics has been immensely enriched by the study of languages which express radically different meaning systems in radically different ways, multimodality would also be much enriched by engaging with cultural diversity. (p. 679)

To understand literacies and multimodality across diverse social and cultural sites, I draw on a mix of complementary theoretical frameworks, each of which is explained in more detail within the individual chapters and projects. What unifies the five chapters are New Literacy Studies (NLS)/literacy as social practice and multimodality/social semiotics, which I see as overlapping theories and approaches to research and learning. Together these theoretical underpinnings and their applications bring a focus to multiple and intersecting contexts of learning in general and how different modes are given meaning and function in social contexts in particular.

New Literacy Studies represent the "social turn" in literacy studies. This tradition of research focuses on what it means to think of literacy as a *social practice* that varies according to time and space but that is also contested in relations of power (Street, 1994; see also Heath, 1983; Street, 1984). In other words, accounts of the uses and meanings of literacies in other places and times are "ideological" in that they recognize the multiplicity of literacy, including whose literacies are dominant and whose are marginalized or resistant (Street, 1984, 2003). Literacy studies need to address how relationships of unequal power shape uses of literacy, who is included and excluded in particular literacy events, and how literacy is achieved in daily life (Baynham, 1995). Moreover, "whichever forms of reading and writing we learn and use have associated with them certain social identities, expectations about behaviour and role models"; individuals "construct an image of an alternate identity for themselves that they associate with the acquisition of a new literacy" (Street, 1994, p. 140). From an NLS perspective, literacy is about knowledge; as Street explains, "the ways in which people address reading and writing are themselves rooted in conceptions of knowledge, identity, and being" (2003, pp. 77–78).

Along with changes in how we understand literacy and what it means to be literate (see also Heath, 1983; Kress, 1997; Lankshear & Knobel, 2003; New London Group, 1996; Street, 1984), there also is growing recognition that there is a qualitative difference in how we communicate through modalities such as the visual, audio, spatial, and linguistic (Kress, 2000, 2003; New London Group, 1996; Stein, 2008) and that different modalities are combined in complex ways to make meaning (Jewitt & Kress, 2003; Snyder, 2001). Similar to NLS, the field of multimodality is concerned with how human beings in various learning environments use different modes of communication to represent or make meaning in the world (Stein, 2008). These modes work in different ways with different effects to create multilayered, communicational ensembles where modes may reinforce each other (i.e., say the same thing in different ways), may have complementary roles, or may be hierarchically structured (e.g., film in which music is foregrounded by the visual [Kress & van Leeuwen, 2001]). As Kress (2003) writes, "It is no longer possible to think about literacy in isolation from a vast array of social, technological and economic factors" (p. 1).

The work represented in this book contextualizes a range of literacies including health, community, family, and multilingual literacies within broader modes of communication (e.g., play and the visual). I view literacy as only one mode of sign-making or communication among many. With its foundation in social semiotics, the domain of multimodality tries to "describe and understand how people produce and communicate meanings in specific social settings be they 'micro' settings such as the family or settings in which the sign-making is well institutionalized and hemmed in by habits, conventions and rules" (Kress & van Leeuwen, 1996, p. 264). A social semiotic perspective views all communication as sign-making and begins with the assumption that as sign-makers, individuals strive for their meanings to be understood maximally in a particular context, which means they must choose the most apt and transparent forms of expression in whatever medium they have at hand (e.g., the use of a cardboard box to make a house). Their interests at the moment of making the sign lead them to choose the most salient aspect or feature of the object or idea being represented. For example, a young child may draw a circle to represent a car if the wheels are taken to be the most salient feature, or a child may say "choo-choo" to represent a train because that sound is the most salient feature of the object.

Methodologically, the studies and examples included in this book bring together ethnography with multimodality and visual methodologies. As Kress has underscored, "Unless we understand the principles of meaning making in all of the ways in which children [and other individuals] do, we won't—so I argue—really understand the ways in which they try to make sense of print" (1997, p. xix). Understanding principles of meaning-making begins with honouring diverse ways of knowing in terms of how we as researchers document practices but also in terms of the modes we make available for participants to communicate their knowledge and experiences. The concept of funds of knowledge, which Moll and Greenberg define as "the essential cultural practices and bodies of knowledge and information that households [individuals] use to survive, to get ahead, and to thrive" (1990, p. 21), broadly frames this work in that it involves first-hand experience with individuals, families, and communities. As such, it affords a powerful way to represent existing resources, competence, knowledge, and ways of knowing, positioning participants in terms of strengths and resources rather than deficits and as informants about their own lives (Hardman, 1973). I consider all modes of meaning-making as intellectual resources and funds of knowledge and take seriously Banks and Morphy's argument that "much that is observable, much that can be learned about a culture [or context] can be recorded most effectively and comprehensively through film, photography or by drawing" (1997, p. 14). They emphasize that neglecting visual data may be a reflection of Western bias (the privileging of the intellectual over the experiential or phenomenological) or overlooking the importance of visual phenomena across cultures, but I extend this argument to all modes. Ethnographic researchers need to recognize that because meaning-making and the encoding of experience takes place in all modes, data collection needs to include a wider range of modes. In a fundamental way, I take inspiration from Kress's strategy to trust my participants and to "try to see by a close look at their actions what I might come to learn" (1997, p. 3) about the principles of meaning-making in a particular social and cultural environment.

All of the work reported on in this book is collaborative in nature. Collaboration takes different forms, including working with colleagues and graduate students but also engaging with individual, families, organizations, and members of various communities. This work has been richly rewarding, built on multiple perspectives that are based on long-term partnerships and networks. Wherever possible, research design began with initial conversations that set the foundation for establishing trust and reciprocity through co-constructed research questions, collaborative data collection and analysis, and research dissemination, including conference and community presentations and publication. Central to collaboration has been capacity building, especially in both Uganda and Kenya. This has included providing research training, experience, and mentorship for local research assistants, such as community members and graduate students at East African institutions (e.g., in research design, interviewing, observing, documenting, and discourse and visual analysis). Whenever possible, we tried to provide opportunities to publish and present in academic venues and secured any necessary funding. We also have provided training for participants and research assistants in the use of digital technology such as cameras, laptops, and voice recorders. In addition, we offered mentorship in writing for young journalist students, community health care for women in rural areas, and domestic and health-care skills for children living in CHHs. Capacity building with the children who were living on their own continued long after our research projects ended and included helping them secure long-term resources and employment opportunities (e.g., through micro loans and small business opportunities such as mobile barber shops and training as auto mechanics). At times, I write from my own perspective, whereas at other times I draw on collaborative projects, so I often move from "I" to "we" at various points in the chapters.

In terms of ethics, all research participants provided informed consent that adhered to the University of British Columbia's research ethics for human subjects. This was not without its challenges, however, particularly in contexts where research participants had limited knowledge of print literacy in general and the practices of university research ethics boards in particular. In all instances, we responded to local protocol for acquiring informed consent and explaining to participants the nature of the various research projects, integral to which was communicating what we hoped to learn and how participation might be beneficial to communities, families, schools, or individuals. At times, informed consent was best secured through oral permission, which was recorded, because of the negative association that signing written documents held in certain communities (e.g., loss of one's land) or because some participants living on their own were too young to provide written consent. At other times, permission first had to be secured through elders or the husbands of women enrolled in a community literacy programme. Pseudonyms are used throughout the book.

The lives of the individuals and groups featured in this book in some ways resonate with my own. As the anthropologist Mary Catherine Bateson writes,

> These resonances between the personal and the professional are the source of both insight and error. You avoid mistakes and distortions not so much by trying to build a wall between the observer and the observed as by observing the observer—observing yourself—as well, and bringing the personal issues to consciousness. You can do some of that at the time of the work and more in retrospect. You dream, you imagine, you superimpose and compare images, you allow yourself to feel and then try to put what you feel into words. Then you look at the record to understand the way in which observation and interpretation have been affected by personal factors.
>
> (1984, p. 161)

As a female university professor, I have lived and worked in a variety of social and cultural contexts, having grown up in a working-class family in a small oil town in Canada. My maternal grandparents were immigrants from eastern Europe and struggled to learn English in their new country. Throughout the writing of this book and in my interpretations of the experiences and perspectives of my participants, I have tried to both "stand inside" the experience from a more empathetic position but also "stand outside" as a somewhat more distant observer, recognizing that research relationships are "complex, fluid, symmetric, and reciprocal . . . shaped by both researcher and actors" (Lawrence-Lightfoot, 1997, pp. 137–138). Although much of the work is collaborative, I take full responsibility for errors in interpretation.

OVERVIEW OF THE BOOK

The broader argument of this book is that powerful pedagogies, methodologies, and theories can be constructed by taking a detailed look at multimodal meaning-making in diverse contexts. By describing and analysing multimodal practices and texts[1] across an array of social learning contexts, the book highlights different constructs, issues, and emerging questions in the study of literacies and multimodality.

Chapter 1 focuses on synaesthetic activity in play as an important context for young children's multilingual literacy learning. I take an up-close look at how Leticia, a young Chinese-Canadian girl, reconfigures her bilingual knowledge of written language through a synaesthetic process that uniquely takes place at home while she is playing school. The example is an illustration of how play can provide a highly productive and liberating context for children to choose the modes, languages, and identities that best suit their immediate learning needs, inquiry interests, and purposes. Leticia's synaesthetic mode shifting and trans-language movement supported her development in all aspects of her semiotic repertoire, including her agency as she constructed real and imagined identities. The narrative she constructs also showcases the kinds of metacognitive, meta/cross-linguistic, and meta-modal conversations that can take place within the context of play and how this might provide a window for teachers and researchers to better understand what is happening as children make meaning through multiple languages, modes, and identities. Play uniquely allowed Leticia to take new risks with her learning while also allowing her to strategize and engage in serious thinking and serious learning conversations. It is worth noting here that it was my own position as researcher and playmate that provided a window on her synaesthetic activity and how it contributed to her language learning.

Chapter 2 continues to explore the relationship between play and multimodality by looking across data examples and field notes from a range of literacy and multimodality studies that I have conducted in Canada and East Africa since 2000. Using four illustrative examples that feature learners across a range of age groups and informal learning situations, I explore how engaging in multimodal role-play provides an opportunity to rehearse and try on a range of identities associated with literacy in different contexts. The focal participants in the three studies include Leticia, who is introduced in Chapter 1, playing "family" as a means of understanding her parents' journey to Canada as refugees from Vietnam; a group of adolescent girls in an after-school journalism club in rural Kenya rehearsing the role of journalist in low-stakes play contexts prior to taking on the actual role in higher-stakes situations; Vincent, an adolescent boy growing up in a child-headed family in rural Uganda playing at being a sportscaster; and women in a community literacy programme in rural Uganda playing the role of "literate woman." The multimodal possibilities of play enable "performance before competence" as learners construct identities that they can perform courageously in low-stakes learning situations of their own making. I argue that the symbiotic relationship between play and multimodality enhances the agency of learners of all ages.

Chapter 3 positions children's images of literacy in relation to current theorizing in multiliteracies, multimodalities, and pedagogical practices in language and literacy. The examples are drawn from elementary school students living in a lower to middle socio-economic class neighbourhood in a city in one of Canada's prairie provinces. The children's images of literacy offer a unique window on their personal and social literacy histories and funds of knowledge. Their drawings showcase the diverse ways that children see themselves and others as literate beings. Although the visual as a mode of representation is becoming increasingly important in communication practices, particularly online, on the whole, the visual aspects of early literacy in classroom contexts remain undervalued (Anning, 2003; Cope & Kalantzis, 2009). In a recent discussion of the role of multimodality in language learning, van Leeuwen (2015) makes a strong case for bringing visual literacies into teacher education programmes. Collecting young children's images of literacy is a starting point for such an agenda. Ideally, the interest in young children's meaning-making through the visual should shift to understanding their communicative practices in general rather than remaining focused on how the visual contributes to understanding print-based learning (Yamada-Rice, 2015).

Chapter 4 concentrates on the affordances and challenges of using visual methodologies in literacy studies. I argue that the increasingly complex nature of literacy in the 21st century requires new ways of accessing the often invisible, accretive layers of literacy practices. Using examples from three literacy studies in Uganda, I demonstrate the potential of visual methodologies for unraveling some of the different constructs, issues, and emerging questions associated with studying literacy in diverse community settings. In each of the vignettes, I use Rose's core visual methodology as a constructive space for the integration of other methodologies to allow for the creation of mixed methods of analysis. Each study blends multimodality and ethnography with relevant theories and methods that foreground the visual as a communicative and cultural resource. The first vignette features two rural schoolgirls' drawings of literacy; the second vignette shows how the visual in HIV/AIDS cartoon messages allows secondary school girls to share a broader range of experiences and knowledge than linguistic modes alone; and the final vignette demonstrates how ecomaps produced by two children in a child-headed family reveal their isolation and limited networks for learning new knowledge. Across these vignettes, I look at what the visual can offer literacy studies, particularly in relation to "thick description" in ethnographic fieldwork.

Chapter 5 extends from the previous chapter on visual and multimodal methodologies into data analysis, specifically in relation to researcher reflexivity. I experiment with Barthes's (1980) notion of "advenience" as a starting point for reflexivity in analysing multimodal texts. Specifically, because multimodality is an emerging and multidisciplinary field that needs to draw on a wide range of different disciplines both theoretically and methodologically (van Leeuwen, 2011), as researchers, we need to be able to account for the diverse modes through which we make and take meaning, including our own performances in them (Byrd Clark & Dervin, 2014). I use the concept of "advenience"—the disharmony between my own interest in an image and the image itself—to situate myself in the analysis of child-created multimodal texts. I propose that identifying what advenes for us as researchers when we view visual and multimodal texts may enable us to think more deeply about how the questions that arise as part of the interpretative process are inextricably linked to our own positionalities, subjectivities, and histories. Reflecting more openly on how we arrive at our research interpretations and how our lives intersect with those of our participants enhances not only our understandings of our participants (and in the process, ourselves), and the issues we investigate, but also the reach and authenticity of our findings.

In the Closing Comments section, I discuss what I think are productive future directions for research on literacy and multimodality: cross-cultural studies, funds of knowledge, inquiry-based learning, and creativity. I consider each of these areas from both a theoretical and a pedagogical perspective, forwarding what I see as new directions that have considerable potential for advancing the field.

NOTE

1. Many of the visual texts that appear in the chapters were produced by children in contexts where paper quality, drawing materials, and writing surfaces made it difficult to reproduce high-quality images on the pages of a book.

REFERENCES

Anning, A. (2003). Pathways to the graphicacy club: The crossroad of home and pre-school. *Journal of Early Childhood Literacy, 3*(1), 5–35.

Baldry, A., & Thibault, P. (2006). *Multimodal analysis and text transcription*. London, UK: Equinox.

Banks, M., & Morphy, H. (Eds.). (1997). *Rethinking visual anthropology*. New Haven, CT: Yale University Press.

Bateson, M. C. (1984). *With a daughter's eye: A memoir of Margaret Mead and Gregory Bateson*. New York, NY: Harper Collins.

Baynham, M. (1995). *Literacy practices: Investigating literacy in social contexts*. London, UK: Longman.

Byrd Clark, J., & Dervin, F. (2014). Introduction. In J. Byrd Clark & F. Dervin (Eds.), *Reflexivity and multimodality in Language Education: Rethinking multilingualism and interculturality in accelerating, complex and transnational spaces* (pp. 1–62). London, UK: Routledge.

Cope, B., & Kalantzis, K. (Eds.). (2000). *Multiliteracies: Literacy learning and the design of social futures*. Melbourne: Macmillan.

Cope, B., & Kalantzis, M. (2009). "Multiliteracies": New literacies, new learning. *Pedagogies: An International Journal, 4*(3), 164–195.

Gee, J. P. (1996). *Social linguistics and social literacies: Ideology and discourse*. London, UK: Taylor & Francis.

Heath, S. B. (1983). *Ways with words: Language, life, and work in communities and classroom*. Cambridge, UK: Cambridge University Press.

Jewitt, C., Kress, G., Ogborn, J., & Tsatsarelis, C. (2001). Exploring learning through visual, actional and linguistic communication: The multimodal environment of a science classroom. *Educational Review, 53*(1), 5–18.

Kress, G. (1997). *Before writing: Rethinking the paths to literacy*. London, UK: Routledge.

Kress, G. (2000). Multimodality. In B. Cope & M. Kalantzis (Eds.), *Multiliteracies: Learning and the design of social futures* (pp. 182–202). London, UK: Routledge.

Kress, G. (2003). *Literacy in the new media age*. London, UK: Routledge.

Kress, G., & Jewitt, C. (2003). Introduction. In C. Jewitt & G. Kress (Eds.), *Multimodal literacy* (pp. 1–18). New York, NY: Peter Lang.

Kress, G., & van Leeuwen, T. (1996). *Reading images: The grammar of visual design*. London, UK: Routledge.

Kress, G., & van Leeuwen, T. (2001). *Multimodal discourse: The modes and media of contemporary communication*. London, UK: Arnold, Hodder Headline Group.

Lankshear, C., & Knobel, M. (2003). *New literacies: Changing knowledge and classroom learning*. Buckingham, UK: Open University Press.

Lawrence-Lightfoot, S. (1997). Illumination: Navigating intimacy. In S. Lawrence-Lightfoot & J. H. Davis (Eds.), *The art and science of portraiture* (pp. 135–182). San Francisco, CA: Jossey-Bass.

Moll, L. C., & Greenberg, J. B. (1990). Creating zones of possibilities: Combining social contexts for instruction. In L. C. Moll (Ed.), *Vygotsky and education: Instructional implications and applications of sociohistorical psychology* (pp. 319–348). New York, NY: Cambridge University Press.

New London Group. (1996). A pedagogy of multiliteracies: Designing social futures. *Harvard Educational Review, 66*(1), 60–92.

Snyder, I. (2001). A new communication order: Researching literacy practices in the network society. *Language & Education: An International Journal, 15*(2–3), 117–31.

Stein, P. (2008). Multimodal instructional practices. In J. Coiro, M. Knobel, C. Lankshear, & D. Leu (Eds.), *Handbook of Research on New Literacies* (pp. 871–898). New York, NY: Lawrence Erlbaum.

Street, B. (1984). *Literacy in theory and practice*. Cambridge, UK: Cambridge University Press.

Street, B. (1994). Cross-cultural perspectives on literacy. In J. Maybin (Ed.), *Language and Literacy in Social Practice: A Reader* (pp. 139–150). Open University.

Street, B. (2003). What's "new" in the new literacy studies? Critical approaches to literacy in theory and practice. *Current Issues in Comparative Education, 5*(2), 77–91.

van Leeuwen, T. (2011). Multimodality. In J. Simpson (Ed.), *The Routledge handbook of applied linguistics* (pp. 668–682). London, UK: Routledge.

van Leeuwen, T. (2015). Multimodality in education: Some directions and some questions. *TESOL Quarterly, 49*(3), 582–589.

Yamada-Rice, D. (2015). Cultural affordances of visual mode text in and of Japanese landscapes and young children's emerging comprehension of semiotic texts. In J. Rowsell & K. Pahl (Eds.), *The Routledge handbook of literacy studies* (pp. 308–321). London, UK: Routledge.

1 “Thinking Like a Child” Synaesthesia, Multimodality, and Multilingualism

In this chapter, I explore how a young child reconfigures her bilingual knowledge of written language when she moves it across modes during play. I consider what we can learn about young children’s meaning-making in general and their multilingual literacy in particular by taking an up-close look at the process of synaesthesia as it takes place during play. I begin by examining some of the ideas associated with synaesthesia in the context of children’s multimodal meaning-making.

SYNAESTHESIA AND MULTIMODALITY

My focus on the intersection of multilingualism and multimodality in young children’s meaning-making is informed by the New London Group’s (1996) “Pedagogies of Multiliteracies” manifesto and Kress’s (1997, 2000, 2003) seminal work on multimodality. The New London Group (1996) coined the term “multiliteracies” to expand “traditional” notions of literacy and to highlight two aspects of the complexity of texts in the contemporary communicative landscape: (1) the increasing salience of cultural and linguistic diversity in a globalized society and (2) the variety of text forms, including those associated with multimodal ways of meaning-making and information technologies.

Multiliteracies scholars have written widely about the changing processes and materialities of text production and interpretation in 21st-century literacy practices (Malinowski, 2014), emphasizing that in any communicative event, language, whether written or spoken, is only partial to the meaning-making process (see, e.g., Kress & van Leeuwen, 1996). As Kress and Jewitt (2003) argue, any given communicative event involves simultaneous modes whereby meaning is realized in different ways by different modes. This multimodal perspective views children as sign-makers who make use of the resources available to them in their specific sociocultural environment. When children engage in meaning-making, they use signs (e.g., language, images, gestures, actions, and objects) to communicate simultaneously the here and now of a social context while representing the resources they have “to hand” from the world around them (Kress, 1997). The sign's intrinsic meanings are not arbitrary but, rather, represent what is central to the sign-maker at that particular moment (Kress & Jewitt, 2003). The meanings also reflect reality as imagined by the sign-maker and are influenced by his or her beliefs, values, and biases. Whereas much has been written about the multiliteracies manifesto in terms of the changing landscape of communication, much less is known about how learners "play with" different sign systems or modes and the "interplay between and across modes," including how one builds on another and how this affords new identities of empowerment in language learning (Kendrick, Early & Chemjor, 2013, p. 397; see also, Early & Marshall, 2008).

A construct central to understanding the interplay between and across sign systems and modes is "synaesthesia," which occurs when one mode invokes another (see, e.g., Kress, 1997). I use Einstein, who attributed his intellectual and creative ability to being able to "think like a child," as an illustrative example of this construct. What does it mean to "think like a child"? In a 2007 article in *Time Magazine*, "It's All Relative: 20 Things You Need to Know About Einstein," Walter Isaacson notes how Einstein's "great breakthroughs came from visual experiments performed in his head rather than the lab. They were called *Gedankenexperiment*—thought experiments" (p. 4). As a 16-year-old, Einstein imagined what it would be like to ride alongside a light beam wondering what would happen to light waves if you reached the speed of light. Would it seem as if they were stationary? He pictured lightning striking at both ends of a moving train. Knowing that math was the language used to describe such wonders, he visualized how equations were reflected in realities. For a decade, he grappled with such thought experiments, the result of which was his theory of relativity. These thought experiments involved moving between and across thinking mathematically, in numbers and symbols, to thinking in pictures, in the visual.

Einstein's ability to "think like a child" required a blending of senses, a translation across modes and systems. This is synaesthesia. It occurs when one mode instigates another, in this case, the visual invoking the mathematical. What is also important to recognize in this example is that cognition has taken place in modes other than language. Kress (1997) insists that we need to uncouple the assumed link between language and cognition and to instead adopt the proposition that cognition is accomplished in all modes. Further, we need to understand cognition and imagination as the same kind of mental activity. Cognition is dependent on the existence of articulations of units and their relations in a particular medium; imagination, in comparison, is dependent on activity moving across media and modes, always going beyond the boundaries set by convention in a particular mode (e.g., poetry extends the boundaries of the linguistic by crossing into sensory modes such as the visual and auditory). Like cognition, imagination operates in all modes. It follows then that meanings also are realized differently in different modes, making it possible to construct analogous meanings in sign systems differing from the mode in which the meaning originally was encoded (Early &

Marshall, 2008). Arguably, this inter-semiotic, ideational meaning-making has generative potential for different cognitive and imaginative engagement. Similarly, Lemke has remarked, "Meanings in multimedia are not fixed and additive (the word-meaning plus the picture-meaning), but multiplicative (word-meaning modified by image-context, image-meaning modified by textual context), making a whole far greater than the simple sum of its parts" (1998, p. 312).

Different modes give rise to different thinking—we constantly translate from one medium to another. According to Kress (1997), this ability, and this fact of synaesthesia, is essential for humans to understand the world. He argues that this activity, this constant work of translation and transduction, is much more strongly present for some than for others, and "seemingly more strongly present for children than for adults" (p. 39). Children's approach to learning is entirely synaesthetic: "Things are always more than one thing, and have different logics, different uses, depending on where you stand when you are looking" (p. 139).

In school, the use of written language typically is fostered over all other modes of expression, particularly as children get older. Yet, as illustrated previously, written language enables only one form of cognition, drawing enables another, and sound and movement enable yet others. Kress's argument is that we need to foster this synaesthetic ability in children's learning rather than suppress it. In other words, we need to allow children to think like children. Children have natural synaesthetic abilities. Rather than building on and extending these, traditional school-based literacy fails to "recognize or adequately use the meaning and learning potentials inherent in synaesthesia" (Cope & Kalantzis, 2009, p. 179). Instead, it tries to corral and confine itself as though written language could operate in isolation from all other modes.

In contrast, play is a system of communication in which many media or modes are used simultaneously, with little or no restraint, and where cognition and imagination merge to become the same kind of activity. In other words, it allows children to naturally engage in synaesthetic learning and discovery. It is a space where children are the "makers and not merely the users of systems of communication" and where they can easily foreground the mode that "feels right" or that is best suited for their purposes (Kress, 1997, p. 163). But even in instances where one mode is favoured, in the brain, there is a continual translation and transduction between and across different modes, even if not outwardly visible (Kress, 1997). This is perhaps why companies like Google and 3M have devised dynamic workspaces complete with toys, slides, and video games that encourage employees to embrace their "inner child" and (re)engage in play. By encouraging adults to relearn how to think like children, these workplaces are intended to stimulate imagination, creativity, and innovation.

In this chapter, I make a case for situating multimodality in general and synaesthesia in particular more centrally within understandings of how young children make sense of multiple languages. In the next section, I introduce Leticia,[1] the focal child in this exploration of multilingual literacy learning, play, and synaesthetic meaning-making.

LETICIA AT HOME AND AT SCHOOL

When I first met Leticia, she was growing up in a multilingual, multiliterate household in an inner-city area of a western Canadian city. Her parents, Howard and Linda Tsiu, were refugees from Vietnam and arrived in Canada as youth during the late 1970s and early 1980s. As parents, they placed a high value on education, and Linda took advantage of programmes and other educational opportunities for parents and children in her community. In fact, I first met Linda when she was participating in a family literacy programme with her six-month-old son, Richmond. Leticia also attended a community English Headstart programme when she was three years old.

Both Howard and Linda spoke Vietnamese, along with English and Chao Chiu, their first language. Both parents also had facility with Cantonese and Mandarin, though to differing degrees. Most often, the family spoke to each other in Chao Chiu and English. Chao Chiu, however, was not typically the language of Leticia's play at home. Instead, she used English with her playmates, who were predominantly her cousins (Ryan and Lily). Wilson, the Tsiu's eldest child, and Leticia were both enrolled in a Mandarin-English bilingual programme at Greencourt Elementary School, a public school 20 minutes by car from the Tsiu's home. Although there were several other public schools in the Tsiu's inner-city neighbourhood, Greencourt was the closest one with a Chinese bilingual programme. The school had a population of approximately 300 students, 40 percent of whom were of Chinese or Vietnamese heritage. At the time of the study, Leticia was enrolled in kindergarten and her brother Wilson was in second grade.

To Howard and Linda, school was serious business, and they expected their children to succeed. They wanted them to learn English in particular, but Chinese as well, because of its importance to their culture. During her kindergarten year, it was expected that Leticia would start reading and writing in both languages. Like most parents, Howard and Linda wanted their children to have opportunities in life. Leticia talked about wanting to be a teacher when she grew up, and her aspirations were encouraged strongly by her parents, who wanted her to develop good work habits and to make high achievements early in her schooling. By December of Leticia's kindergarten year, it was their hope that she would already be reading. Leticia was keenly aware of her parents' expectations and tried in her own way to garner their approval.

Linda also had a number of other expectations for her daughter's language and literacy learning. One of her primary concerns involved English and Chinese writing. She often would write sentences and request that

Leticia sit at the kitchen table and copy them. In one scribbler, for example, English sentences such as "I am a girl" and "I go to the mall" were written by Linda and sporadically—with a tentative hand—copied by Leticia. Chinese characters were particularly difficult for Leticia, and Linda often reproached her for not being able to write her Chinese name correctly. Over time, considerable tension appeared to develop around reading and writing, reaching a point where Leticia regularly refused to work with her mother. Midway through the kindergarten year, Linda became so concerned with her daughter's education that she enrolled her in a subsidized Montessori school for two afternoons per week. This new arrangement meant that Leticia attended kindergarten for five mornings and Montessori school for two afternoons a week. In time, the kindergarten teacher began to complain that Leticia was having difficulties concentrating and focusing at school.

At school, Leticia also made particular choices about how she would participate in literacy activities. Colouring worksheets, which are typical kindergarten fare, almost always elicited the same lackadaisical response. At home, colouring met with the same response, even with the assortment of crayons, markers, and colouring books that she had. She was interested in storybooks, though, and listened intently when stories were read aloud in kindergarten (and at home). She also enjoyed looking at books during the scheduled times in the kindergarten and often shared pictures with whoever was sitting next to her during shared book reading. Both her parents and teacher thought she should put more effort into her written work at school, especially her Chinese (writing her Chinese name remained a challenge for the duration of her kindergarten year). English printing and speaking came much more easily to her. In fact, Miss Lee, Leticia's kindergarten teacher, described her as one of the stronger English speakers in the class. Her Mandarin, however, was assessed as average.

As children enter school, they are confronted with trying to understand who they are in relation to their teacher and classmates and with merging their home identity with their school identity (Miller & Mehler, 1994). Children also must come to understand who they are in relation to literacy at school (Solsken, 1993). How Leticia accomplished these tasks in terms of the two languages she was learning and how she encountered the discourses embedded in both her home and school environments became important questions in understanding her meaning-making in general and her multilingual literacy in particular.

DOCUMENTING LETICIA'S MEANING-MAKING AT HOME

For well over a year, my life was interlaced with the lives of Leticia and her family. To understand this young girl's meaning-making, I observed, participated in, discussed, and audiotaped events within the contexts of her home and classroom. I adopted the unique dual role of playmate and researcher.

My role as playmate enabled me to enter Leticia's meaning-making world in a way that would not have been possible had I remained an outside observer. As a player in, rather than merely an observer of, her multimodal activities, I was better able to understand the meanings she attached to actions and objects. Our play relationship fostered a deeper and more intimate connection between researcher and participant—a relationship that I believe enhanced productive inquiry in this study. As Lawrence-Lightfoot (1997, pp. 137–138) emphasizes, "Relationships that are complex, fluid, symmetric, and reciprocal—that are shaped by both researcher and actors—reflect a more responsible ethical stance and are likely to yield deeper data and better social science." As both playmate and researcher, however, I recognize that my roles were by no means neutral ones. Kelly-Byrne (1989, p. 206) argues, "The myth of the neutral researcher and the much-desired objectified research account have made it both mandatory and possible to ignore the human reality of the research relationship, in all its chaos and with its many foibles." When we research human lives, our own lives as researchers inevitably become entangled in the lives of our participants, just as their lives become entangled in ours; it is the complexity and subjectivity of that entanglement that enhances and promotes the richness and authenticity of qualitative research.

In general, the qualitative field research procedures that I used were in the tradition of those outlined by Barton and Hamilton (1998), Heath (1983), Philips (1983), Taylor (1983), and Taylor and Dorsey-Gaines (1988) in their classic sociocultural studies of family and community literacy and Goodwin (1990), Kelly-Byrne (1989), and Sutton-Smith (1980) in their observational studies of children's play. More specifically, I utilized a variety of research procedures, including combinations of observations and interactions within the context of the home, local neighbourhood, and Leticia's school; conversation records; and artifact collection. Observations always took place within the everyday, routine activities of the family and classroom and were never staged.

Leticia's play interactions at home were audiotaped using a small, handheld tape recorder. Observations of her interactions with family members and friends, at home and in the community, were recorded as handwritten field notes. Classroom observations were also recorded in writing. Interviews with family members were very much conversational in nature, often taking place at the kitchen table over tea or dinner and never adhering to any formal structure. These open-ended conversations were valuable in interpreting and analysing Leticia's activities. Detailed accounts also were made of the forms and functions of print in the home as well as Leticia's writing endeavours at school. The content and function of written materials used by the family were an important resource for understanding Leticia's approach to literacy, both in English and Mandarin.

My aim in interpreting Leticia's play was to better understand the principles of her meaning-making (Kress, 1997) in relation to her literacy learning.

As I observed activities at home, at school, and in the community, I made connections between the detail of her meaning-making and larger structures of the play narrative's overall meaning in relation to the context of Leticia's life. These connections helped me develop inferences (i.e., interpretive hypotheses) about their broader significance in Leticia's life. Finally, through interpreting the data with the family, I attempted to come to some conclusion about how the story's meaning might be a reflection of Leticia's own family culture, social history, and language and literacy practices. My goal was to ascertain how the play episodes, what I refer to as "play narratives," might be indicative of the stories that Leticia was telling herself about herself (Geertz, 1973), her interests as a sign-maker, and her principles of meaning-making.

This chapter is part of a larger study comprised of 10 play narratives selected from the 30 home visits recorded during the year I spent with Leticia and her family (see Kendrick, 2003). I include two play narratives about playing school. The first narrative serves to illustrate the tensions between Leticia and her mom that had emerged over time in relation to reading and writing expectations at home. I juxtapose the second narrative with the first to show how moving meaning across symbol systems and modes in synaesthetic play activities generated new understandings of literacy in general and Mandarin in particular. Each narrative is examined as a communicative event comprised of multiple and simultaneous modes of representation including symbolic action, language, gesture, and image. I have incorporated my interpretation of Leticia's use of these modes into a multilayered narrative account.

Playing School

Narrative 1: "Miss Lee Just Lazy"

It was 4:30 on a cold December afternoon, and at this time of day, Leticia almost always stopped whatever she was doing so that she could watch Pokémon with her older brother Wilson. Today, I joined Linda in the kitchen, while she prepared supper. When the programme was over, Leticia decided that she wanted to play school. She took the file folder that I had given to her mother to collect her writings and drawings and opened it on her lap. She removed her Chinese printing scribbler from the folder and asked me for my pen. Everyone in the living room (her mother, two brothers, and me) was told to sit down on the carpet so that she could take attendance.

> "I am Mrs. Hai,[2]" she announced. "Who are you?" she asked Wilson.
>
> Wilson was experimenting with different Pokémon names, and he practiced writing them on his hand. He would show his hand to Leticia to see if she could guess his name. She was unsuccessful in reading them, and he took great delight in this. Of the two names that he had written, Pokémon and Pikachu, he chose Pikachu.

"Richmond is Yee-Yee, and my name is Pee-Pee," Linda said, giggling. Leticia laughed at the names. "My name is Leticia," I told her.

"Okay," Leticia said and began to take attendance. "Pikachu?" There was no response from her brother.

"Pikachu?" she said again, with volume and impatience.

"You're supposed to say *I am here*," I whispered to Wilson.

"Yeah," Leticia scolded.

"No," he retorted. "I am not Pikachu. I am Leticia, too." Both he and Leticia laughed. She continued to call the names of her students. Each time we responded with "I am here," she made a check mark in her book next to a squiggle that she had made to represent each student's name. The baby was having trouble sitting still and crawled determinedly over to Leticia to get her folder. Linda and I kept pulling him back, and tried to encourage him to sit on one of our laps. Using her best "teacherese," Leticia scolded, "Yee-Yee, you're supposed to listen!"

After taking attendance, Leticia decided that her name was not going to be Mrs. Hai but was Mrs. Lee[3] instead. Linda, although she had gone into the kitchen to feed the baby, continued to participate in her daughter's game.

Leticia pointed to her older brother and me, "Leticia and Leticia can go down to the office. Do you know where's the office?" she addressed me in particular. I shook my head no, and she pointed to the bathroom door in the hallway. "There's the office. You take the attendance there."

"Tomorrow, Yee-Yee and Pee-Pee can go to the office," Leticia noted.

Wilson temporarily went back to watching TV, and when I returned to the living room, Leticia handed me a paper from her file. On it was a drawing that I had made of her Christmas keychain when we were playing earlier in the afternoon.

"You need to colour this," she told me. "Just pretend!" She seemed fretful when my pen almost touched the drawing.

"Do you have a snack? It's snack time." I shook my head no. She moved me over to the table beside the sofa and pretended to bring back cookies.

"Thank you, Miss Lee."

"It's not *Miss* Lee. It's *Mrs.* Lee," she said with annoyance, then announced, "Now, I read a story." She searched through her public library book bag for a story to read and removed two books. "Today, I'll read this one. Tomorrow, I'll read this one," she said.

"Teacher, I want to read the *Ginger Man* book," her mother called from the kitchen. Leticia looked through the bag for the book. When she found it, Linda said, "Yeah, yeah, that one," and commented to me, "she can read it."

"This is Mrs. Lee's new book," Leticia began, holding the book in front of me so that I could see it from where I was sitting on the floor.

She looked over at her mother and baby brother and tried to get the baby's attention, calling "Yee-Yee! Yee-Yee!"

"Yee-Yee, listen to the teacher," Linda told the baby.

Leticia held the book up so that we could all see the pictures and began to tell the story. "The *Gingerbread Man.* A little old man and a little old woman had a son. Then some children come to their . . . What's this?" She pointed to the next word in the sentence.

"House," I told her.

"House," she continued. "The little old woman said (she pointed to the word *said*) I'm going to make you something to eat." Leticia was struggling to remember the exact words for the story and had a hard time continuing.

"The teacher is lazy," her mother commented from the kitchen when Leticia was unable to continue. "Can Leticia move closer? She cannot listen to you," she asked, seemingly hoping that if I sat closer, Leticia would allow me to help her read the story.

"I don't want to read it. I don't remember," she said quietly, looking down at the floor.

"Oh, you're doing a good job! You're a good teacher," I said in an effort to encourage her to continue.

"I don't remember. I only know this letter," she told me, turning to the back of the book. Showing me the words *Then SNAP!* She read them with great expression then closed the storybook. "Um, Mrs. Lee cannot read this now. Mrs. Lee forgot to read. Mrs. Lee don't remember."

"You just lazy. Miss Lee just lazy," Linda said, laughing from the kitchen.

"Nooo," Leticia said sadly, avoiding her mother's gaze, and then snapped harshly, "It's not *Miss* Lee. It's *Mrs.* Lee!"

"You just lazy." Her mother's words hung in the air–

"Nooo!"

"She tried really hard last night, the teacher," Linda said with pride. "She sat there [at the kitchen table], and she read it by herself."

"Did she?" I remarked.

"She tried really hard!"

Commentary

At the heart of this play narrative are Leticia's interests as a sign-maker: the role of a teacher and storybook reading. I include this narrative for two reasons: First, it makes visible many aspects of literacy that this young girl has mastered; second, it highlights some of the tensions between what Leticia can do with literacy and what her mother expects her to be able to do.

The episode begins with light-hearted humour as we choose names for the students we will play in Leticia's classroom. Linda chooses Pee-Pee for herself and Yee-Yee for Ryan. Although the rhyming names have a distinctly

Chinese sound, Linda and Leticia laugh at the English interpretation of *Pee-Pee*. Wilson cannot decide between the names Pokémon and Pikachu, which are characters from his favourite television programme. He teases Leticia by writing the names on his hand, perhaps enjoying his status as the older brother and the fact that his younger sister cannot read these names yet. I choose the name *Leticia*, wondering how she will respond to me in her role as the teacher. Following my announcement, Wilson also decides to take the role of Leticia. Leticia, who initially adopts the name of the educational assistant in her kindergarten classroom, quickly changes her status by appropriating her teacher's name with one modification—she insists on being called *Mrs.* Lee rather than *Miss* Lee. She emphasizes this distinction each time she is referred to as *Miss* in error, which, like many of her play narratives focused on family life, reveals the importance she places on the status of marriage.

The morning routine of taking attendance follows with Leticia-as-teacher carefully using check marks and other notations to record who is present and who is absent from the classroom, a classroom practice that she gives importance to and that she has painstakingly observed. During this routine, Leticia insists on silence and cooperation from her students. When Yee-Yee, her baby brother, does not comply, she scolds, "Yee-Yee, you're supposed to listen!" in the authentic tone and language of a teacher. With similar authority, she directs Leticia and Leticia to take the attendance to the office. It is early in December, and Leticia already knows the culture of her kindergarten classroom; she knows the procedures for talking like a teacher, taking attendance, scheduling time for a snack, assigning work, and reading a story. In this play episode, story reading is Leticia's primary interest. Although she has chosen her own book, she is uncharacteristically open to her mother's suggestion that she read the *Ginger Man* book, perhaps because she is in role and the context is playful. Linda listens intently from the kitchen and encourages Richmond to "listen to the teacher."

Leticia begins her story reading by building a sense of excitement about the book. "This is Mrs. Lee's new book!" she tells her students with enthusiasm. She positions the book so that the pictures and text are visible from her students' perspective and turns to the first page of the story. She begins to retell the story in her own words. She knows how to vary her voice and tone to create drama and interest in the story. Her ability to read the exact words in the story, however, is still emerging. Knowing implicitly her mother's expectation that she try to read exactly what is written on the page, she struggles to identify each of the words. In her attempt to both retell the story in her own words and read the exact words on the page, the two methods conflict, and attempts at word reading prevail. There is a clear tension between the skills Leticia is able to display and her mother's expectations percolating below the surface of the narrative. When Leticia is no longer able to continue reading the story, Linda becomes frustrated, asserting, "The teacher is lazy" because she believes her daughter has the ability but is not putting in the effort to read. As a strategy, she suggests I move closer to assist her daughter with reading, but Leticia already has abandoned the book "reading." She is honest with her "students," though, and does not attempt to save face, confessing instead, "Mrs. Lee cannot read this now. Mrs. Lee forgot [how] to read. Mrs. Lee don't remember." Linda's repeated comment, "Miss Lee just lazy," causes Leticia to lash out at her mother with "It's not *Miss* Lee. It's *Mrs.* Lee!" in what is perhaps a futile attempt to exert her status and power as the teacher. Linda tries unsuccessfully to encourage her daughter to continue by explaining to me that Leticia was able to read all of the words in the book last night. Leticia predictably refuses, and our play episode ends in disappointment and frustration.

Narrative 2: The Sea Animal Big Book

This second play episode took place several months after "Miss Lee Just Lazy." Like many of the other home visits, this episode began with our retreat into the basement to play so that we wouldn't wake Richmond during his afternoon nap. As we descended the stairs, Leticia lifted her arms in the air, indicating, as a small child might, that she wanted to be picked up and carried. This gesture was a clear sign that she wanted to "play mommy." I lifted her into my arms, carried her downstairs, and sat her at the table. The family room, which was usually very neat and tidy, was somewhat dishevelled today; the tabletop had loose-leaf pages and markers strewn across it. These materials seemed to provide inspiration, and suddenly Leticia changed her mind about what she wanted to play. "I'm Miss Lee. You are Mrs. Hai," she announced as she got up from her chair and stood by the small whiteboard mounted on the wall.

> "I'm going to make the morning message. You do the newsletter," she directed, picking up the four dry erase markers that she had connected end to end exactly the way Miss Lee did in the kindergarten. She removed the cap from the black marker, and tried to write on the whiteboard, but had some difficulties because the marker had dried up. She tried one marker after the other in an attempt to write the morning message but abandoned them and chose instead to stack the loose-leaf sheets into neat piles on the table. Picking up one of the stacks, she asked, "Can you help me staple this?"
>
> "Do you want to staple it like a book with three [along the side] or one here [in the top left corner]?" I asked.
>
> "Um, one . . . Okay, these are their work, and they can do anything they want," she said, referring to the children in her classroom. I collected my field notebook from my backpack, and as I was opening it, a small paper book about sea animals[4] fell out. The book consisted of several photocopied pages stapled together. Miss Lee had given it to me for my files the last time I visited the school.
>
> Leticia immediately recognized the book from school and gasped, "You took that home?"

"Miss Lee gave it to me," I explained.

"Okay," she replied more cheerfully, taking the book from my hand. "I'm going to copy this, okay? I'm going to copy this. Make a big book."

"Oh, you want to make a big book."

She added more sheets of paper to the booklet that she made previously and brought it to me to staple, this time along the side "like a book." She was very insistent that I not put any staples through the holes of the loose-leaf sheets.

"Now I'm going to make a book," she said excitedly. "I'm going to copy it" (see Figure 1.1). She then looked carefully, and somewhat apprehensively, at the detailed pictures and the Chinese print and asked, "Can *you* copy this for me? Can you? Can you copy this for me?"

"Do you want to do some of it, and I'll do some of it?" I suggested in an attempt to scaffold her participation in writing.

"No. You draw right there," she said, referring to the middle of the first blank page in her book, "and I will draw right there." She pointed to the top of the same page.

"So do you want me to write the title?"

"No, I want to write it."

"Okay, that's what I thought."

She took my black marker and started copying the English title of the book.

"S," she said, and continued with the name of each letter as she wrote it on the page after instructing, "You spell the word."

"E-a and then a space and a big A-n-i-m-a-l-s," I directed. "There you go."

"*Sea Animals*," she read as she ran her finger under the title.

I pointed to the English word below the title and asked, "Do you know what this word says?"

"No," she said somewhat sheepishly.

"That says *name*."

"Oh yeah," she responded with relief. "Put the name," she said to herself. "Name," she repeated as she printed the word.

"Did you read this book to your mom last week?" I asked, remembering Miss Lee's instructions to the kindergarten students.

"I didn't take that book home yet."

"No? But I thought that you were supposed to read it when your mom came to school [for parent teacher interviews]."

"Yeah, I didn't do that."

"You could take this one and read it to her today," I offered.

"I need to write the Chinese," she said to skirt my suggestion and then carefully copied the first Chinese character in the title.

"You're a very good printer," I commented as I watched her print the character.

"I need my sunglasses," she said suddenly.

Figure 1.1 Sea Animal Book Cover

“Are they where your mommy is in the kitchen?”

“No, in my room.”

“In your room?”

“Can you go get it? It’s too little.”

“So, do you mean that you need your sunglasses to see the Chinese writing?”

“Go get it. Go, go, go, go, go, go, go.” She hurried me out of the room.

“It’s on your desk?” I asked from the stairs.

“Yep.”

I went upstairs and brought back her sunglasses, which she promptly put on. She had written all six of the Chinese characters in the title (see Figure 1.1).

“Read this!—*Hai*,” she said excitedly.

“*Hai*,” I repeated after her.

“*Yang.*”

“*Yang.*”

“*Dong.*”

“*Dong.*”

“*Wu.*”

"*Wu. Hai yang dong wu.*"

"*Wu,*" she repeated, correcting my pronunciation.

"What do you want me to do now?"

"Do all the pictures. There's the picture right here (on the cover)."

"Do you want me to trace it?"

"Yeah, I'm going to teach the kids, okay?" She rearranged the chairs around the table so that she could try again to write on the whiteboard with the dried-out markers. "Miss Lee has new markers. Mommy said she's going to buy me new markers." I suggested that we tape a piece of paper to the whiteboard so that she could use her other markers to "teach the kids."

As I was taping the paper to the whiteboard, she suddenly noticed that I had been tracing the picture from the cover of the book.

"You know what my dad said. You shouldn't trace."

"You shouldn't trace, right?" I asked, assuming the house rules don't apply to me.

"*You* too!" she corrected somewhat indignantly.

"I know, me too."

"You have to use your imagination. You *don't* copy."

"What if I leave what I've done and I draw a real picture?"

She looked again at what I had traced. "No, trace it."

"No, I'm going to draw it for real," I replied.

"No, put it in [the book under the loose-leaf page], and just trace it."

"I thought Daddy said that wasn't a good thing to do."

"Just you can trace. Not us," she said, attempting to persuade me.

"I shouldn't trace either."

"*You* can trace—only big people."

"I know how to draw, too. Can I show you?" I tried to convince her of my drawing talents.

"No, just put it back."

"Watch, I can look at it and draw."

"No, I don't want you to." I carefully drew part of the picture, and Leticia seemed suddenly reassured that the drawing would not be spoiled. She watched me drawing as though mesmerized. "Are you concentrating?" she asked. I nodded, showed her the picture, and asked her what I should draw next.

Pointing to one of the small fish in the centre of the picture, she said, "That one."

I drew the fish as she watched intently. "Draw that starfish," she directed, comparing the original with my drawing to determine whether I was missing any of the little details.

"The hardest part about doing this is the Chinese writing," I commented. "Do you think that writing in Chinese is hard?"

"Hmm?"

"I do. It's hard for me. Is it very hard for you?"

"No."

"Do you think that you're a good artist?"

"I don't know. Sometimes."

"Is it better that I'm not tracing the picture?"

She nodded her approval and commented on my drawing, "That's a poison fish."

"It's a jellyfish. . . . Do you think that I'm doing a good job, though?"

"Yeah." Together we finished drawing the picture. Leticia consistently chose to draw aspects of the picture that were simple and easy to copy. The more complicated figures were either left for me to complete or for us to negotiate about who would draw what.

"I don't want to draw that," she said, pointing to a sea plant.

'You want me to draw that? Do you want to do the lines on it?"

"No. . . . Yeah, I want to," she said, taking a second look at the drawing.

"You do?" I was somewhat surprised and watched her interest as she drew the lines. "That looks perfect," I told her. We continued to fill in the details of the picture and then moved on to the next page.

"You do that," Leticia said, pointing to the Chinese characters. "I'll do that." She was referring to the English sentence "*This is a blue whale*" (see Figure 1.2).

Figure 1.2 Blue Whale Page

"Okay, you want me to write the Chinese, and you'll do the English. Do you want to write the English first?"

"Yep."

"Okay." She carefully printed *This a blue whale*, omitting the word *is*. She then read the sentence above it in Chinese: *Zhè shì yi tou lan jing.* She used her best "teacherese" and waited for me to echo what she had read. I followed her lead and repeated what she had read.

"What's that?" she asked, referring to the circle at the end of the Chinese sentence.

"That's a period."

"It's like this?" she asked, pointing to the English period.

"Yeah, but it looks different in Chinese." I began writing the Chinese sentence. "Miss Lee can write so fast—even Mrs. Hai. I'm so slow," I complained.

"Do you wish you were Superman?" she asked in a serious tone.

"Do I wish I were Superman?"

"Yeah, you're a hero."

"A hero?"

"Yeah."

"I wish I could talk Chinese."

"*I* can talk Chinese," she emphasized.

"Now we have to draw [the blue whale]? Which parts on this picture do you want to draw?"

"The killer whale and the dolphin and the fish," she said, flipping through the book and pointing out all of the remaining pictures she wanted to draw. "You draw the crab. I'll draw the shark." She outlined who would draw each of the pictures and consistently assigned the more complex and difficult drawings to me.

"I want to do that [the English sentence]," she continued and began neatly copying the words from the book.

"You're good at that. Now I'll do this one [the Chinese text]. Does this say *people*?" I asked, referring to one of the characters in the Chinese sentence.

"Umhm," she confirmed.

"I wonder why it says . . . What does it say? The whole thing?"

"*Zhè shì yi tou shi ren jing,*" she read.

"I wonder why it has *people* [i.e., *ren*] there?" I carefully printed the Chinese characters, while Leticia watched. "Do you want to do the period at the end?"

"Yeah." As she printed, she said the sea animal names in Chinese, *lan jing, ren jing.*

"*Jing* means whale?"

"Yep, it's whale. This is a killer whale," she said, reading the English sentence.

I try to translate the Chinese sentence into English. "In Mandarin, *yi* is the word for both *one* and *a*? This is *one* killer whale?" I asked as I read the Chinese characters in English.

"Yeah. This is *one*," she confirmed.

"Are these two [characters] *blue*?"

"That's *blue*," she pointed to one of the characters. "See, *lan*, that's *blue*."

"Oh, *lan* is blue." I finished writing the sentence in Chinese.

Linda and Richmond joined us downstairs to see what we were doing.

"Who drew this?" Linda asked, looking at the cover of the book.

"We did it together," I explained. "Leticia drew this [the killer whale], and I drew this [the blue whale]."

"She copied? She put it on top?"

"No, she drew it herself. This one [the cover] she drew all of the smaller detail stuff."

"That is nice!" Linda responded with uncharacteristic enthusiasm.

"I'm going to take it school tomorrow and show Miss Lee," Leticia told her mother.

"Do you want to read it to Mommy?" I asked, expecting her usual "no." Instead, she began to read the first two sentences to her mother.

"Oh, really good," praised her mother. Leticia continued to draw the picture of the dolphin as her mother observed.

"You just look at the picture and draw it?" Linda asked.

"Yeah."

"Yeah," Linda commented to me, "I think that she is better at this than Wilson."

As we moved to the next page and I began to write the Chinese characters, Leticia told me, "Do it quickly. You need to learn to write fast 'cause you're slow."

"I know. How could I get faster?" She looked at me but didn't respond.

"Look! We got no more pages!" she gasped when she realized that we were only part way through copying the book and had only two pages left.

"We can add more on. How many do we need?" I asked.

"Okay, count how many pages I need."

"Um, five," I answered. She counted out five loose-leaf sheets, and we stapled them to the back of our book.

Commentary

This play episode, which took place a few months after the first episode that I describe in this chapter, shows a change in how and why Leticia engages in both Chinese and English literacy across languages. What has shifted from the first example? An up-close look at Leticia's communicative and representational resources, particularly as they intersect and build on one another, make visible how her interests as a sign-maker, her identity as a language learner, and the synaesthetic activity within a particular space of learning are all important factors in widening opportunities for representation and communication.

As a kindergarten student figuring out how to navigate the rules and routines of school, Leticia's interests as a sign-maker often turn to the roles and responsibilities of teachers in the classroom; this narrative begins with determining what our roles and responsibilities will be in this co-constructed story. The materials and resources available in Leticia's home environment factor into how she constructs the role of teacher, and her school history with literacy tools in particular emerge as key components of what Miss Lee does in the classroom. She has watched for many months now her teacher's use of dry erase markers for writing the morning message, and these are especially important to her in her own role as teacher. The whiteboard, papers, staplers, and "work" for students are also literacy tools associated with Miss Lee's position and authority within the school context. When Leticia sees the *Sea Animal* book fall out of my notebook, she gasps, "You took that home?" expressing the distinction she makes between literacy items that belong at school and literacy items that belong at home. The realization that I have Miss Lee's permission, though, appears to ease her concern, and our play activity becomes focused on producing a "big book" to match the smaller one.

Leticia is initially very excited about creating the big book until she begins to examine the Chinese and English text and the pictures in the book. Her request, "Can you copy this for me," signals, as it has in other contexts, that copying the text and the pictures on her own will be too difficult. At first, she assigns "Mrs. Hai" (the educational assistant) the responsibility. Her reaction to me tracing the pictures in the book reveals the expectation of her parents, particularly her father, that she use her imagination instead of tracing. Although learning to draw is emphasized more for Wilson than for Leticia, it is important to both Howard and Linda that their children use all of their abilities to excel in school. Similar to her response to printing the Chinese characters, Leticia appears to question her drawing ability and is reluctant to engage in a task that may not be a success. As we work through drawing the picture, first by tracing and then free hand, her confidence increases, and she becomes more willing to explore her own drawing capabilities. She gradually immerses herself in copying selected portions of the text and pictures. She first initiates writing the title of the book in English, obviously feeling confident enough to print *Sea Animals* as I dictate the spelling. As we move from the title to the word *name* on the cover of the book, though, she becomes somewhat reluctant when she doesn't immediately recognize the word. Once reminded, she continues with an increased level of confidence.

An increasing level of confidence is an integral factor in this book-making activity, which marks one of the first instances at home or at school where

I observe Leticia choosing to write Chinese characters. After printing the title in English, the word *name*, and the first of the six Chinese characters in the title, she seems to need time on her own away from the watchful eyes of an adult. After announcing, "I need to write the Chinese," she requests that I get her sunglasses upstairs. This private period creates an opportunity for her to work through writing the rest of the Chinese characters, and when I return with her sunglasses, she has printed all six of the characters in the title. She excitedly launches into teaching me how to read what she has written; I repeat each word after her and follow her corrections in my pronunciation. The characters she has written are well formed on this first page (see Figure 1.1). When compared with the characters she has written in Figure 1.3, a page produced near the end of the book making, there is a curious difference in her penmanship.

Her fine motor control proved to be a barrier in the past and integral to her refusal to write her name in Chinese. In the first example, I did not observe Leticia write most of the characters. In the second example, I watched as she loosely structured lines to form the last two characters. The

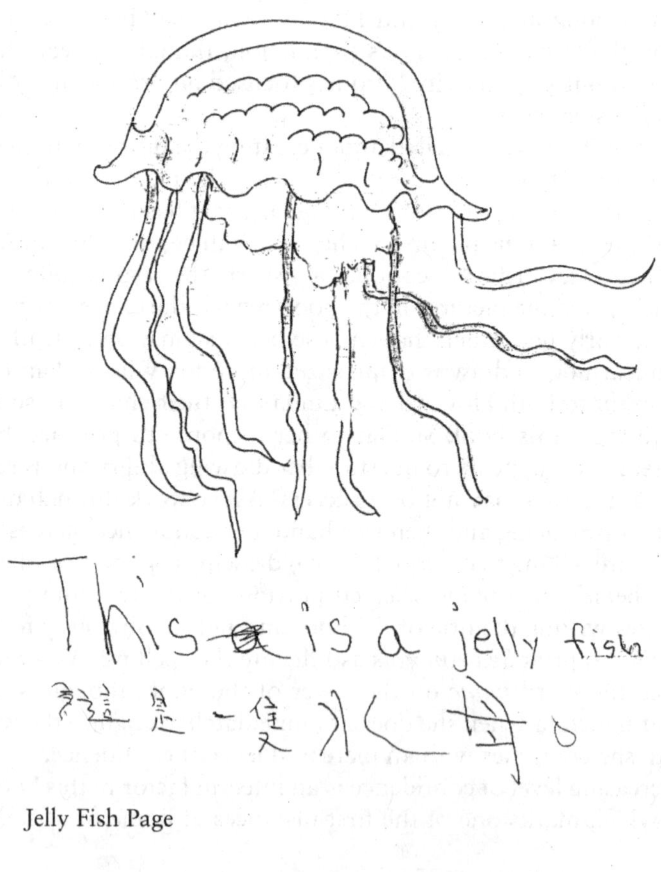

Figure 1.3 Jelly Fish Page

first five characters in the sentence *This is a jelly fish* were written by Wilson at Leticia's request (see Figure 3.1). The characters are quite complex with considerable detail, and she was unwilling to attempt them on her own. Yet several of the characters in the title are equally complex. How has Leticia managed to write these? I speculate that she may have traced the characters, a strategy that works with detailed drawings but not one that she seems to have tried with the Chinese characters. We have in previous situations discussed my approach to writing Chinese characters where I try to look at the characters as images and try to copy them as an artist might.

As the play episode unfolds, we continue to work back and forth across the pictures, the print in English and Chinese, and oral language both in and out of role, interweaving and building meaning across modes. Leticia watches intently as I undertake drawing the sea animals, then she begins writing the English sentence *This is a blue whale* to accompany the corresponding image. From here, she shifts readily to Chinese, reading aloud *Zhè shì yi tou lan jing* in Mandarin with little hesitation. Our discussion of the characters in this sentence outside of the play roles (e.g., my questions about the meanings of the characters) provides another opportunity for Leticia to take on the role of authority as she solidifies her own understandings by shifting meanings across Chinese, English, and the visual, both in and out of her play role. Our status here is somewhat equal as we are both learning to read and write in Chinese. We are able to talk freely about the challenges we both faced in learning to write in Chinese and in learning to draw. My process in many ways parallels her own, and seeing me struggle may have created a safety zone in which she was willing to show her own vulnerabilities as a learner, something she would never have displayed in school or at the kitchen table with her printing book. It is possibly this slowing of time and collapsing of space and movement across symbol systems in the liminal play context that makes visible for her the similarities and strategies in our processes.

At school, Leticia did not use spoken or written Chinese as frequently as many of the other students, relying instead on her knowledge of English; I was therefore surprised by the confidence with which she approached teaching me how to read in Mandarin. As the teacher, Leticia appeared far more willing to risk making mistakes, perhaps because she knew that no one was going to correct or reproach her. In this role, she is dominant, whereas I am subordinate as student or educational assistant; we have played these roles many times, and she knows that as a subordinate, I will neither criticize nor correct. The context of play provides a safe environment in which she doesn't need to concern herself with meeting parental or teacher expectations. Her position of control and power as the teacher in particular here seems to give her the confidence to undertake literacy activities that she refuses to engage in as a subordinate student in the classroom or a subordinate daughter at the kitchen table. The two Chinese characters at the end of the sentence in Figure 1.3 were written in the role of teacher and, surprisingly, in the presence of Linda and Wilson.

As we progress in making the book, Leticia is feeling so confident with her ability that she complies with my suggestion to read some of the book to her mother. Linda too is quite amazed at both her daughter's reading and drawing. She responds with uncharacteristic enthusiasm to Leticia's hand-made book, stating, "I think she is better at [drawing] than Wilson." Leticia is obviously very proud of the book we have made, and as usual, she wants to take it to school to "show Miss Lee." Connecting her world at home with her world at school is of obvious importance to her perhaps because it allows her to bring together two sets of expectations, her teacher's and her parents', in relation to her own developing literate identity.

In making the book, when Leticia directs me to print the Chinese characters, I am slow and methodical, and when I express my lack of confidence, she responds with, "Do you wish you were Superman?" Her comment is an intriguing one, and it is obvious that she associates speed with Superman and his powers. At school, Leticia is as reluctant to use Chinese print as she is at home. Activities, for example, that involve using both English and Chinese texts often are completed with only the English text. Her Chinese printing scribbler at school contains characters that are written quickly, but not carefully, and Leticia is sometimes asked to rewrite what she has written. She similarly casts me as a struggling student when she reprimands me as I print the Chinese characters, saying, "Do it quickly. You need to learn to write fast 'cause you're so slow." Her statement "*I* can talk Chinese" in this play episode and her statements "We Chinese people" and "We Chiu Dana people" in other episodes, reveal a possible tension between her strong identification with her Chinese culture and the difficulties she experiences with Chinese literacy. As Cope and Kalantzis (2009) emphasize, learning to write in any language requires forming an identity. Although some learners can comfortably and confidently work their way into that identity, others who may be more like Leticia cannot. Such learners need opportunities to extend their communicative repertoires beyond writing alone into synaesthetic activities such as play, which are more intellectually stimulating and motivating than copying sentences or letter–sound correspondences.

*****

The case study example of Leticia offers a lucid illustration of how play can provide a liberating context for learners to make judicious choices about which modes, languages, and identities they want to draw from and under what conditions. Leticia's synaesthetic mode shifting and trans-language movement supports her development in all aspects of her semiotic repertoire, including her agency as she constructs her real and imagined identities. Relatedly, the narrative she constructs also showcases the kinds of metacognitive, meta/cross-linguistic, and meta-modal conversations that can take place within the context of play and how this might provide a window for teachers and researchers to better understand what is happening as children make meaning through multiple languages, modes, and identities. Play uniquely allows her to take new risks with her learning while also allowing her to strategize and engage in serious thinking and serious learning conversations. It is worth noting here that it is my own position as researcher and playmate that provides a window on Leticia's synaesthetic activity and how it contributes to her language learning. This is perhaps an unusual position for a researcher to occupy but from an ethnographic perspective, it gives me permission to enter this young girl's social world so that I can better understand her meaning-making practices from an inside perspective. Together, we co-construct this narrative, negotiating symbol systems and languages in authentic activity and conversation.

On a final note, I want to draw attention to this example as evidence of how young children use play in their home contexts to recontextualize and build on their background knowledge from school both in terms of content (e.g., *Sea Animals*, realized bilingually and visually) as well as the practices and positions taken up in schooling. Bernstein's (1996) notion of "recontextualization" as a social perspective "makes evident how discourses that originate outside of education" (in this case play narratives) are "realized in a manner apt for a specific pedagogic site, its audience and its purposes, to constitute the content of school subjects (Bezemer & Kress, 2008, p. 169). Leticia built on texts, tasks, and practices and, in occupying her "teacher identity," became the designer and orchestrator of her own learning. For this young multilingual language learner, much is to be gained from changes of mode within the context of play.

NOTES

1. Names throughout this chapter are pseudonyms.
2. Mrs. Hai is the name of the educational assistant in her kindergarten.
3. Miss. Lee is the name of her kindergarten teacher.
4. This teacher-made book is a dual-language book written in both English and Chinese.

REFERENCES

Barton, D., & Hamilton, M. (1998). *Local literacies: Reading and writing in one community*. New York, NY: Routledge.

Bernstein, B. (1996). *Pedagogy, symbolic control and identity: Theory, research, critique*. London, UK: Taylor and Francis.

Bezemer, J., & Kress, G. (2008). Writing in multimodal texts: A social semiotic account of designs for learning. *Written Communication, 25*(2), 166–195.

Cope, B., & Kalantzis, M. (2009). "Multiliteracies": New literacies, new learning. *Pedagogies: An International Journal, 4*(3), 164–195.

Early, M., & Marshall, S. (2008). Adolescent ESL students' interpretation and appreciation of literary texts: A case study of multimodality. *Canadian Modern Language Review, 64*(3), 377–397.

Geertz, C. (1973). *The interpretation of cultures*. New York, NY: Basic Books.

Goodwin, M. H. (1990). *He-said-she-said: Talk as social organization among Black children*. Bloomington: Indiana University Press.

Heath, S. B. (1983). *Ways with words: Language, life, and work in communities and classroom*. Cambridge, UK: Cambridge University Press.

Isaacson, W. (2007). It's all relative: 20 things you need to know about Einstein. *Time Magazine*. Retrieved from: http://content.time.com/time/specials/packages/article/0,28804,1936731_1936743_1936781,00.html

Kelly-Byrne, K. (1989). *A child's play life: An ethnographic study*. New York, NY: Teachers College Press.

Kendrick, M. (2003). *Converging worlds: Play, literacy, and culture in early childhood*. Bern, Switzerland/New York, NY: Peter Lang.

Kendrick, M., Early, M., & Chemjor, W. (2013). New literacies in a rural Kenyan girls' secondary school journalism club. *Research in the Teaching of English, 47*(4), 391–419.

Kress, G. (1997). *Before writing: Rethinking the paths to literacy*. London, UK: Routledge.

Kress, G. (2000). Multimodality. In B. Cope & M. Kalantzis (Eds.), *Multiliteracies: Learning and the design of social futures* (pp. 182–202). London, UK: Routledge.

Kress, G. (2003). *Literacy in the new media age*. London, UK: Routledge.

Kress, G., & Jewitt, C. (2003). Introduction. In C. Jewitt & G. Kress (Eds.), *Multimodal literacy* (pp. 1–18). New York, NY: Peter Lang.

Kress, G., & van Leeuwen, T. (1996). *Reading images: The grammar of visual design*. London, UK: Routledge.

Lawrence-Lightfoot, S. (1997). Illumination: Navigating intimacy. In S. Lawrence-Lightfoot & J. H. Davis (Eds.), *The art and science of portraiture* (pp. 135–182). San Francisco, CA: Jossey-Bass.

Lemke, J. L. (1998). Metamedia literacy: Transforming meanings and media. In D. Reinking, M. C. McKenna, L. D. Labbo, & R. D. Kieffer (Eds.), *Handbook of literacy and technology transformations in a post-typographic world* (pp. 312–333). Hoboken, NJ: Taylor & Francis.

Malinowski, D. (2014). Drawing bodies and spaces in telecollaboration: A view of research potential in synaesthesia and multimodality, from the outside. *Pedagogies: An International Journal, 9*(1), 63–85.

Miller, P. J., & Mehler, R. A. (1994). The power of personal storytelling in families and in kindergartens. In A. Haas Dyson & C. Genishi (Eds.), *The need for story: Cultural diversity in classroom and community* (pp. 38–54). Urbana, IL: National Council of Teachers of English.

New London Group (1996). A pedagogy of multiliteracies: Designing social futures. *Harvard Educational Review, 66*, 60–92.

Philips, S. U. (1983). *The invisible culture: Communication in classroom and community on the Warm Springs Indian Reservation*. New York, NY: Longman.

Solsken, J. W. (1993). *Literacy, gender, and work in families and in schools*. Norwood, NJ: Ablex Publishing Corporation.

Sutton-Smith, B. (1980). Children's play: Some source of play theorizing. In K. Rubin (Ed.), *New directions for child development* (pp. 1–15). San Francisco: Jossey-Brass.

Taylor, D. (1983). *Family literacy: Young children learning to read and write*. Exeter, NH: Heinemann.

Taylor, D., & Dorsey-Gaines, C. (1988). *Growing up literate: Learning from inner-city families*. Portsmouth, NH: Heinemann.

2 Imaginative Play, Multimodal Meaning-Making, and Literate Identities

Several years ago when my son was very young, we were playing at the beach with toy cars, driving them over sand and logs and jumping them across gaps between rocks. He became deeply engaged, taking on the identity of his car, Lightning, giving it a voice, and playing out actions and interactions in an unfolding narrative. The play was sustained for well over two hours with limited moments of stepping out of role. It was one of the first times I can remember him engaged in imaginative play. As the play progressed, he became increasingly more adept at manoeuvring his car and matching his language and voice to the context and situation, using vocabulary and expressions that I had not previously heard him utter. When we finally left the beach and were driving home, my son made the comment, "I can't stop being Lightning." For me, this was a profound statement, a metacognitive realization that he had been playing someone other than himself, a statement made as though he were "beside" himself or seeing himself from another perspective, transported beyond himself to the point that he almost believed he actually was the car (Huizinga, 1950/1955).

Imaginative play has the unique ability to carry one across time, space, and entity. Its role in human development and culture has long been studied by philosophers, anthropologists, psychologists, educators, and the like, yet the vast majority of this work has focused almost exclusively on young children. Looking across data examples and field notes from multimodal studies that I have conducted in Canada and East Africa since the mid-1990s, I have been struck by the importance of imaginative play across a range of learning contexts, not only with young children but with adolescents and adults as well. In this second chapter, I explore what happens to learning when the affordances of multiple modes are harnessed in imaginative play. I begin with four reflective examples from studies with learners ranging in age from early childhood to adulthood. The first reflection shows how imaginative play provides an important forum for a young Chinese-Canadian girl to begin to make sense of and retell family history. The second reflection shows the critical role of imaginative play for adolescent girls in Kenya to rehearse the future role of journalist, including the use of new digital technologies. In the third reflection, I consider how imaginative role-play is an important tool for an adolescent boy as the head of his household in rural Uganda to entertain, share in-the-moment news and information, and nurture family relationships with his younger siblings. In the final reflection, I focus on women enrolled in a community literacy programme and the ways in which pretending to be a "literate woman" enhances their investment in their own literacy learning. The next section provides a starting point for thinking about imaginative play in relation to multimodal meaning-making.

MULTIMODALITY AND PLAY

Multimodality is concerned with "how human beings use different modes of communication, like speech, writing, images, gesture, and sound to represent or make meaning in the world" (Stein, 2008, p. 871; also Kress, 1997; Kress & van Leeuwen, 1996). In *Before Writing,* Kress demonstrates how in learning literacy, young children use a range of modes to express their meanings in play. In this chapter I argue that it is not just young children, but rather learners across all ages, that rely on the affordances of imaginative play in their multimodal meaning-making.

Integral to both play and multimodality is social semiotics, a theory that attempts to explain how signs are used to "produce and communicate meanings in specific social settings" (Kress & van Leeuwen, 1996, p. 264). Signs simultaneously communicate the here and now of a social context while representing the resources players and learners have "to hand" from the world around them (Kress, 1997). Players use signs and modes simultaneously to create an event or product, whether these have complementary roles, are used to reinforce each other by saying the same thing in different ways, or are ordered hierarchically, where one mode is dominant over another (Kress & van Leeuwen, 2001).

Play, like multimodality, is everywhere. It is one of the most fundamental elements of human culture. As humans, we have an instinct for play, and this instinct has nurtured achievement across the arts and sciences in profound ways. According to Huizinga (1950/1955), the whole of human culture emerged out of the capacity to play and to adopt a ludic attitude either in a contest *for* something or a representation *of* something.

All play takes place within a marked space—whether a real playground or metaphoric one. It is a well-defined activity that is outside of "ordinary" life. When players step out of their everyday worlds, they move into a higher order. Such performances are filled with imagination whereby the player is consumed with "making an image" of something different, something other than their reality (Huizinga, 1950/1955, p. 14). In other words, play is based on the manipulation of certain images—on a certain "imagination" of reality. It is a projection of an interior life onto the world, a way of transforming the world according to what we imagine (Bruner, 1983). This conversion of reality into images and images into actions requires a constant transduction across modes, what Kress (1997) refers to as "synaesthetic activity." Play, because of its combinatorial nature, encourages synaesthetic activity through experimentation with various signs, tools, and modes for meaning-making. It is a kind of experimental test frame—a "hot house" for combining thought, modes, and imagination in never-before-seen ways (Bruner, 1983).

One of the fundamental qualities of play is that it implies a reduction in the seriousness of consequences of errors and setbacks (Bruner, 1983). Bruner describes a social experiment whereby he and colleagues studied young children engaged in a game that required retrieving coloured chalk from a box that was situated some distance away from where they were sitting. The rule was that they could not move from their seats, but they could employ various materials such as sticks, clamps, and string. They divided the children into three groups. The first group was allowed to play with the materials before having to complete the task. The second group was given a "pedagogical demonstration" explaining how you could make a longer stick by joining shorter sticks with a clamp. The last group simply was familiarized with the materials and given a few demonstrations of what each material was like. All of the children had the same amount of exposure to the materials. Not surprisingly, the children who had a chance to play with the materials beforehand were able to solve the problem much faster.

Similarly, in "Learning by Design: Good Video Games as Learning Machines," Gee (2005) examines how video game designers are able to get new players to learn long, complex games. He argues that good game designers trigger learning by building in good principles of learning. Among these principles are "sandboxes" and adopting an identity. In the real world, sandboxes are "safe havens" for children yet still look and feel like the real world. Using the term metaphorically, Gee explains that sandboxes are good for learning because if learners are put into a situation that feels like the real thing, but with risks and dangers greatly mitigated, they can learn well and still feel a sense of authenticity and accomplishment. Play is an activity that provides a unique courage, or as Vygotsky put it, "In play a child always behaves beyond his average age, above his daily behaviour; in play it is as though he were a head taller than himself" (1978, p. 102).

At its best, play is a way of exploring complex situations and alternative perspectives (Huizinga, 1950/1955). This deep learning recruits an extended commitment when players take on a new identity in which they are heavily invested. When learning involves playing a character, for example, in a science classroom, learning works best if students think and act like scientists. Investment in new identities or roles can become powerful motivators for new and deep learning in a variety of learning contexts (Gee, 2003). Moreover, as Holland, Lachicotte, Skinner, and Cain (1998) observe, when players make up worlds through play, they engage in a serious process of identity making. In play, children "tell others who they are, but even more importantly, they tell themselves and then try to act as though they are who they say they are" (Holland & Lave, 2001, p. 3). In other words, play is "a story the players tell themselves about themselves" (Geertz, 1973, p. 237).

When players take on a role or character in make-believe play, there is an opportunity for them to perform a new identity in a context that allows for risk-taking and error making without real-world consequences. Cazden (1981) describes such learning as "performance before competence," which takes place within a learner's zone of proximal development, "the distance between the actual developmental level as determined by independent problem solving and the level of potential development as determined through problem solving under adult guidance or in collaboration with peers" (Vygotsky, 1978, p. 86). I use Cazden's learning principle to further consider the possibilities for pairing play and multimodality and the particular types of contexts and conditions that enable performance to precede competence. The assisted performance contributes to subsequent learning.

What follows are reflections on four examples from a range of studies in Canada and East Africa that show what happens to learning when imaginative play is the context for multimodal meaning-making: retelling family history as a cumulative cultural text, the liminal space of a journalism club, remixing oral traditions, and playful performance in a women's literacy programme. My intention here is to put diverse examples in conversation together to look for patterns and possibilities for better understanding play as integral to multimodal learning.

Reflection 1: Leticia's Cumulative Cultural Text From Canada to Vietnam

This first reflection[1] features Leticia, who I introduced in Chapter 1. She is a young Chinese-Canadian girl growing up in a multilingual household in a western Canadian city. I focus here on the intersection of play and multimodality as this young child interweaves memories of family history with her everyday lived experience into a "cumulative cultural text," what Weber and Mitchell (1995) describe as a build-up over time of cultural constructions. Her play narrative as a multimodal, cumulative cultural text reveals traces of family history accumulated through shared stories, photographs, and videos and used as meaning-making resources in the present as a means of retelling and making sense of a complex family history. To contextualize Leticia's text construction, I begin with a recount of her family's story of immigrating to Canada, as told to me by her parents, Linda and Howard, during the year-long ethnographic case study that I conducted in their home. Both were from ethnic Chinese families that were living in Vietnam and fled during the mass exodus in the late 1970s to early 1980s.

Linda's family left Vietnam in 1978 when she was a teenager. They had to pay a significant fee for each of the 10 family members who made the journey. With few financial resources remaining, Linda's mother sewed jewellery into the hems of her children's clothing to ensure the family's survival once they arrived in a new country. Linda explained that her parents hoped the hidden jewellery would not be discovered should pirates invade. For the entire month spent on board the boat, Linda recalled that the lack of water was most difficult. With more than 300 refugees on the boat, food was rare, but water was almost none existent. Families resorted to bartering, trading jewellery, and cigarettes—anything for drinking water, which was never fresh and typically collected in rusty basins and containers. Vacant space on the boat was as scarce as water, with passengers being limited to a small seat where, for 30 days, they sat, slept, and ate. The boat finally docked in Indonesia, and it was here that the family awaited news from the United Nations about a country that would be willing to accept them as refugees. They remained in Indonesia for a relatively short time—a total of three months—before learning that Canada had agreed to take them as new immigrants and that a family was willing to sponsor them. Their point of arrival was a rural area of Manitoba, where the 10 family members were very fortunate to remain together. They lived in a farmhouse for several months and were assisted by their sponsors to adapt to Canadian life, including learning English.

Being able to communicate in many languages was something that Howard valued greatly, perhaps because he believed his own language abilities saved his life when he fled from Vietnam in the early 1980s. He told me of the pirates who raided the boat he was travelling on and explained that they would surely have killed him had he not been able to communicate with them. According to Howard, because there was some degree of commonality between his language (Chao Chiu) and the language of the pirates, he was treated relatively well and given privileges such as water, food, and even cigarettes. He spoke openly of other difficulties he had endured when trying to flee his war-torn homeland. As the eldest son in his family, he took the risk and responsibility of escaping Vietnam with the hope of finding a safe place to bring his parents and siblings. He was candid about not being able to afford the large fee for passage on a refugee boat. Determination led him to illegally organize a small refugee boat that would carry some 20 passengers. The fact that he was caught and imprisoned for four months only to reorganize the day he was released from prison speaks eloquently of his ingenuity and commitment to family. Once in Canada, he held three jobs, so he could afford to bring other family members to Canada.

The year prior to when I met Leticia and her family, Howard took several weeks of holiday to travel back to Vietnam with his parents. This trip marked his first return since he left in 1980, and he commemorated the occasion by making a video to share with Linda and the children. Leticia had never flown on an airplane, but she had been to the airport to say goodbye to family members. She had never been to Vietnam, but she talked about visiting Vietnam with her father one day. When Howard returned home, he had numerous gifts and promised that he would never travel without his family again because he missed them so much.

Both parents worked hard to provide a strong family and upbringing for their children, who were the heart of their home. Although they also wanted their children to know the sacrifices they made in choosing to immigrate to a new country, they felt the children were still too young to fully understand their stories of coming to Canada. Howard, though he wasn't one to complain, sometimes talked with frustration about his own family's lack of understanding. "Before they came to Canada, they just thought the streets were paved with gold. They had no idea that I was living in a rooming house, scrimping and saving every penny so that I could afford to bring them to Canada." When Howard's parents and younger siblings arrived in Canada, they moved into a suite that he had furnished with a colour television, beds, a table and chairs and had stocked with food. He said that even after being in Canada all these years, he still didn't think that his siblings had a true understanding of what it was like for him to journey by boat from Vietnam and struggle to survive his first few years in Canada.

Linda lamented that she was unable to read English newspapers when she first came to Canada. She wanted to know the stories that were told about the Vietnamese refugees. From microfiche, I collected articles from the *Globe and Mail* and the local newspaper to share with her. She carefully preserved them and intended to give them to her children when they were older. At the time that I met her, Leticia only had fragmented pieces of her parents' stories, pieces that she had just begun to weave into the fabric of her own life, as evident in the cumulative cultural text, co-constructed with me as her playmate, which follows.

> "Come on, Daddy," Leticia said as we were leaving the house. We pretended to walk out to the car with our bags and suitcases. Leticia was using a birthday gift bag, given to me by her family, to carry her blanket.
>
> "Okay," I said when we got to the car, "put the bag in the trunk." I sat down in the driver's seat of the car [the left side of the picnic bench in the basement].
>
> "No, Daddy's driving, Mom. You can't drive," she explained.
>
> "I can't drive?"
>
> "No, you have a baby [in your tummy]."
>
> "Oh, okay."
>
> "Daddy, come on. You sit with me, okay?" she said to me.
>
> "Okay, move over," I said to the people who we pretended were sitting in the back of the car. "Who's coming with us?" I asked Leticia.
>
> "All the families live with us.[2] All the families [are] coming with us. Come on, Wendy.[3] Come on, Grandma. Come on, Grandpa. I'll sit on your lap [said to me]. Grandma and Grandpa sit at the front with Daddy."
>
> "Is it a long trip?" I asked.
>
> "No, we have to take a airplane," Leticia told me.
>
> "Oh, we have to take an airplane?"
>
> "We're here. Come on, Grandma. Come on, Mom," she said. "Here you take these [the gift bag]. Take all the suitcases."

"Have you got everything?" I asked.

"I helped you."

"Okay. Now?"

"Our auntie's going to say bye-bye to us. Bye Uncle, bye Brian, bye Auntie." She waved to the other family members.

"Bye." I waved along with her. "Where's the airplane?" I wondered aloud. She asked me to hold the bags that we had packed and set about building an airplane. Using the four chairs from the table, she made a row. In front of the first chair, she took a footstool with a round base and turned it upside down. The base of the stool resembled a steering wheel. "That's for the driver," she informed me.

"Have you been on an airplane before?" I asked as I watched her make the airplane.

"Daddy. Daddy has."

"Where do you want me to sit?"

"At the front," she said.

"At the front? Okay. You have to put the suitcases under the seat."

"You sit there with Grandma," she told me. "Oh, what about Grandpa? Here comes Daddy! Daddy drives the plane."

"Daddy drives the plane? Where are we going?"

"Banff . . . and Vietnam."

"When we get off the airplane, where will we be?"

"Banff," she explained and then suddenly said, "we need to go home."

"We need to go home?"

"Yes, we need to get stuff for Banff, and we need to get a card from Vietnam."

"We're going to send a card from Vietnam?"

"Come on, Mom, all our stuff's there."

"Do you need your blanket?" I asked, carrying the gift bag with the blanket back to the house.

"No, Vietnam is hot," she reminded me. We left the blanket in the house and pretended to collect other materials before returning to the airplane.

"Okay, ready?" I asked. "Tell me when we're there. Is it going to take a long time to get there on the airplane?"

"No, we're almost there," Leticia explained.

"Oh good. What are we going to do in Vietnam?"

"Just buy stuff. We're going to send it home."

"You're going to send it from Vietnam?"

"Where did you bought that teddy [a panda bear that I gave her]?"

"In–"

"San Diego?" She finished my sentence.

"San Diego."

"What did you saw there?" she asked.

"I saw the zoo, and I saw the ocean."

"And what?"

"And I saw some stores and . . . I went to [a conference] there."

"And what?" Directing my response, she added, "You bought some stuff there from some stores."

"Yes, and I bought some stuff at the zoo."

"Let's go to Vietnam and buy some stuff," she suggested.

"Where are we staying in Vietnam—in someone's house or in a hotel?"

"In a hotel. Okay, let's buy some stuff." She walked around the room looking for things to put into her bag. "I want to buy something for Uncle," she told me.

"Okay."

"Maybe we could buy this [a tin box]," she decided.

"What is it?" I asked.

"Open it."

"Do you think Grandma would like that?"

"It's for Auntie," she informed.

"Where do we pay for it?"

Leticia walked over to where her father's desk calculator sat and pretended to key in some numbers. "Do-do-do-do, done. Put all the stuff that we bought in the bag [my gift bag]. I'm going to buy this coat for Brian [her cousin]."

"Are you buying stuff for everyone who came to the airport to say goodbye to us?"

"No, it's for teacher too. I have to write this for teacher," she said, showing me a folder.

"Oh, you have to write what you did on your trip for teacher?"

"Yeah. This is a good folder. And this [a box of Kleenex] for, um, for the teacher. We need to go."

"Are we going home from Vietnam, or are we somewhere else?"

"It's night-time," she reminded me. "We need to sleep. Where's Daddy?"

"He's gone to sleep."

"I'm going to sleep, 'kay. Goodnight."

(PLC transcripts: Session 21)

In conversations and interactions that I shared with Leticia during our year together, she often referred to stories her father told her about his trip back to Vietnam and China. She also told her mother that she wished their "whole family" could go on a "big camping trip." Rowsell and Pahl point out that, "As children come to write [construct texts] the host of experiences they have had since birth are brought to bear on the writing processes," and we need to "question the way texts come into being" (2007, p. 402). Moreover, we need to track "discursive and multimodal patternings within texts. There is a complex relationship between the author of a text and the environment in which it was made" (2007, p. 402). The text that Leticia constructs represents her accumulated family history, which includes her parents' stories of leaving and returning to Vietnam, her memories and desires in her own family life, and her cultural understandings of these.

When Howard took several weeks' holiday to travel back to Vietnam with his parents, the trip marked his first return since he left in 1980. He commemorated the occasion by making a video to share with Linda and the children. He also returned home with numerous gifts. In constructing this narrative, Leticia has obviously been influenced by her father's stories and experiences. She has never flown on an airplane, but she knows that at the airport, family members often come to say goodbye. She also knows how to stow her baggage safely under her seat. She has never been to Vietnam, but she knows that it is hot and that she will not need her blanket. Leticia talks about visiting Vietnam with her father one day, and she tells me that they are going to cross the water in a yellow boat, a boat that he has shown her on video and in photographs.

Visiting Banff is also interwoven into Leticia's family history. A recent family holiday was a trip to Banff National Park that she made with her immediate family, her maternal grandparents, an aunt, an uncle, and a cousin. The trip was made over a long weekend just before school started because Linda and her sister wanted the children to have something to write about when they were asked about their summer holidays when they returned to school. Buying special things for family members is also a salient part of Leticia's story in the final part of this narrative. In consultation with her mother, she takes the important responsibility of finding gifts for family members: something for Uncle, Grandma, and Auntie, a coat for her cousin Brian, and a box of Kleenex for her teacher.

The disparate elements of Leticia's embodied narrative form a "cumulative cultural text," which draws on Fiske's (1991) ideas on intertextuality and the ways readings of a primary text (in this case Leticia's parents' stories) and secondary texts (Leticia's play narratives) "leak into and inform each other" (Mitchell, 2014, p. 89). Through the use of multiple modes such as embodied language, gesture, and action, Leticia was able to write herself into her parents' stories of coming to Canada. She takes what is most appealing, what is most familiar, and weaves this into her own embodied story. She creates a sense of belonging and identity, imagining herself travelling with many family members, perhaps the way her mother had as a young girl escaping Vietnam, and merging this with elements from her father's recent return to Vietnam, transforming images and words into her cumulative cultural play text. Play and multimodality are integral aspects of this text because they allow her to test out story lines, ideas, identities, modes, and practices in a low-stakes environment. This "hot house" becomes a place where she can experiment and nurture her own identity and life story, writing her own family history and gathering elements from the past to define both her present and her future.

Reflection 2: Play in the Liminal Space of a Girls' Journalism Club in Kenya

This next reflection was part of a collaborative study[4] focusing on contextual issues of situated writing practices in an after-school journalism club in rural Kenya. We documented how 32 girls (age 14–18 years) used local cultural and digital resources (i.e., donated digital cameras, voice recorders, and laptops with connectivity) in both playful and authentic ways in becoming young journalists. In foregrounding context, we drew on the concept of liminal spaces, together with notions of placed resources, New Literacy Studies, multiliteracies, multimodality, and identity work. The learning space of the journalism club was an important transitional space for the girls to take on the identity of journalist. They used situated rehearsal, appropriation, and performance of the roles and linguistic repertoires that they associated with competent journalists, housed in underground forms of play. The findings suggest that engaging in particular kinds of "play" and "performance" opened untried possibilities for the girls to engage with new literacies and acquire new, more confident and professional identities and develop new writing practices. The following extracts from conversations illuminate the ways in which the students emphasized how their competence as journalists took time and required opportunities to rehearse and authentically play the role of journalist, complete with the "role-clothings" (see, e.g., Sutton-Smith, 1959) of digital camera, voice recorder, and "press badge."

The girls attended a residential secondary school in a rural area of Kenya. Many of their parents were subsistence farmers or pastoralists. Prior to their participation in the journalism club, the girls had had very limited exposure to digital tools and online resources. The school was quite under-resourced by Kenyan standards, a factor that the teachers believed inhibited the girls' academic performance. Regardless, government exams dictated the curriculum and limited the students' ability to engage in low-stakes learning opportunities that were more typical of an after-school club. In the two part reflection included here, I show how imaginative play and multimodal meaning-making enabled experimentation with new tools, practices, and identities in highly productive ways in learning to become young journalists.

Part 1: Looking Like a Journalist

Maureen: Why do you think these devices [the digital camera and voice recorder] gave you access to important people [e.g., local politicians], access that you didn't have without the devices?

Asha: When we have the recorders, we can be simply compared with those professional journalists, so we are journalists in short.

Mary: If we have the devices, we cannot just take the devices alone. We take up the [press] badges, like the ones we were having yesterday, the one that is for reporters.

Maureen: Okay. So you look like a journalist?
All: Yes.
Maureen: And did you feel right away as soon as you started using these things—I am a journalist—or did it take time?
Mary: It took time.
Asha: For me, and the rest of my colleagues, it was our first time to use the devices. Then another thing that was challenging, it is when you want to interview somebody [a classmate], but she is not willing to give out all the information. So at times we were forced to hide those devices for the sake of information.

In her final statement, Asha is referring to how, in learning to use the digital voice recorder in particular, they resorted to hiding it in the sleeves of their sweaters so that they could record their classmates without their knowing. This "underground" journalism was necessary, in their opinion, so that they could learn to use the devices in an authentic way. They explained that learning to be a journalist involved practicing interviews, and they tried to do this with classmates during leisure time at school. Unfortunately, because their classmates had never seen a digital voice recorder, they did not always readily agree to be recorded, so at times the girls pretended to be underground journalists to avoid intimidating their peers. This playfulness, this particular form of pretend, make-believe play, allowed the members of this journalism club to create "possible roles in possible worlds" (Dyson, 1997, p. 14) in a space where the imagined identities of journalists could be appropriated prior to adopting the actual identity. Of significance is the opportunity to test new tools and new identities within a play-based context. Sutton-Smith (see, e.g., 1959), in his seminal research on play, stresses the significance of "role-clothings" (e.g., the digital recorder, camera, and press badge) in aiding players' abilities to take on unfamiliar roles in make-believe play. The girls used these role-clothings in pretend—albeit secret—interview contexts as embodied rehearsals that enabled them to later take on roles as "real" journalists, as they gradually gained entry into this professional community of practice.

We also discovered recordings on the voice recorder of the girls in the club pretending to be television anchorwomen, and in the next example, the girls describe the importance of these role models in learning to become journalists.

Part 2: Role Models

Gift: Okay, for me, I am looking upon my role model for example, Kanze Dena—a presenter in Citizen TV. Now, I used to look at what she is doing, and now I just follow what she is doing.
Maureen: Okay. So you have a role model?

Gift: Yeah.
Maureen: Who else has a role model? What kinds of role models do you have?
Nancy: A reporter.
Maureen: A reporter on TV?
Nancy: Yeah. Her name is [Terryanne] Chebet.
Maureen: Also on Citizen TV?
Nancy: Yeah.
Mercy: Me, my role model is Maimuna Ali . . .
May: Mine is a news reader on Citizen TV . . .
Maureen: So most of you have role models on some TV [channel]?
All: Yeah.

We view the appropriation of the identities of these TV personalities, as performed and recorded by the girls in the learning space of the journalism club, as a kind of make-believe play critical to more fully understanding the authentic role of a reporter. The "club" was an in-between space, a space that was neither constrained by the mandated curriculum of the classroom nor the expectations of the culture of professional journalists. In this liminal space, social relations, rules, and expectations underwent ludic recombination in ways that would not have had a place in the everyday lives of these girls. This recombination set the stage for taking on new discourses and practices in their interviews as their topics and interviewees expanded from familiar, local audiences to an international, online women's rights magazine where some of the girls published articles later in the study.

Reflection 3: Vincent's Remix of Oral Traditions

This third reflection is taken from a study focusing on the use of multilingual cultural resources among children living in child-headed households (CHHs) in Uganda's Rakai District.[5] We documented children's everyday agency as they worked and played together, spotlighting their use of stories, songs, riddles, and proverbs as tools for teaching and learning with siblings at home. Here, I reflect on a specific example that demonstrates how play as integral to multimodal oral tradition becomes a means for Vince to entertain his younger siblings and share news and information they would not otherwise have access to. Vince is 17, the second eldest of five children living together on their own. He has one older brother, Gerald (age 18), and three younger siblings, Lawrence (age 16), Jane (age 13), and Michael (age 10). Their parents died of AIDS, and when we first met the family, they had been on their own for approximately four years. Without financial resources, and with the added responsibility of caring for his siblings, Vince was unable to continue his schooling and began to assist his older brother Gerald with subsistence-level coffee crops. The three younger children were in school at the outset of the study. The family also earned money by assisting with cattle rearing for neighbours. All five lived in a mud house on a small plot of land that belonged to their parents.

The children in our study co-constructed, reappropriated, and remixed oral traditions such as stories, songs, riddles, and proverbs in situated ways for purposes specific to the changing contexts of their lives. Many of them created their own riddles and co-constructed understandings as a means of entertaining their siblings. Others were highly inventive at devising their own storytelling practices at home. Vince's approach was particularly creative and playful because he liked to communicate with his brothers and sister through role-playing sports news. As he explained:

> Another way we communicate is through sports. Since childhood, I have been a fan of soccer, so I usually tell them [my siblings] the teams that are going to play. For instance, today Arsenal is going to play against Liverpool and Aston Villa vs. Newcastle. I always give them updates; for instance, Manchester United will play against Middlesbrough at 7:00 p.m. I try to update them about soccer that will take place over the weekend.

Given their very limited resource base, this young family did not own a radio, and whenever Vince had reason to go to the trading centre for odd jobs, he took the opportunity to catch up on the latest news about British soccer. When he said that he tried to "update" his siblings about the latest soccer news, what he did was deliver the news by adopting the imaginary role of sportscaster. His in-role commentaries were anticipated eagerly by his siblings and not only provided entertainment and news of the global world of soccer but also served as an important way of maintaining sibling bonds and relationships and the practice of telling oral stories. This new way of "storytelling" as a sports commentator was a kind of imaginary play for Vince, whose love of soccer and engagement in make-believe was also expressed in the act of writing *Manchester United—Manager* on the front door of his family's new World Vision house, which they moved into at the end of our study. His storytelling via role-play is a hybrid model of both an indigenous form of communication and contemporary radio communication (Mushengyezi, 2003). The play-based practice both preserves the traditional way of passing on information and values while also localizing global news.

Vince's imaginary identity was a purposeful performance in the context of a "remix" on oral storytelling that is much more than words alone. Intermingled with "the array of other communicative modes of which verbal language is only one" (Finnegan, 2007, p. 210), his sportscasting is a playful, multimodal performance that is "a form of action, of art and of reflection" (p. 1) in everyday practice. As Peek and Yankah (1994) eloquently observe, all oral traditions (remixed or otherwise) are windows on "the exchange of life through words" (p. xii), just as music and art are. They refer to creative speech and verbal arts in many African cultures as vital forms of expression for communicating values, beliefs, and practices. Vince's creative and playful ways with words makes visible an "imagined identity" (Kanno & Norton, 2003), a rare instant when all else is suspended—poverty, loss, and worry—in a moment of laughter, imagination, and hope. Without their parents, this family must now navigate their future on their own, with Vince taking on a role that is both father and brother. He does this as a child too soon becoming an adult, escaping into play and using it artfully to guide, entertain, and bond with his siblings in this new role to soothe, however temporarily, their disrupted lives.

Reflection 4: "Not Being a Cartoon" and Rural Ugandan Women's Literate Identities

This final reflection was part of an ethnographic study on literacy practices and local modes of communication in three rural Ugandan communities (for further details, see Kendrick & Hissani, 2007). The larger study documented the communicative practices of 15 women, ranging in age from 22 to 53, who were enrolled in an adult literacy programme in the West Nile area of Uganda. The women initially learned literacy in Alur, the local language, with the possibility of later progressing to English. In this area of Uganda, and among the participants, women's daily activities revolved primarily around domestic responsibilities; most had married at a young age and had children and husbands to care for, and all had very limited formal school experience. Oral and performance traditions such as storytelling, singing, and dancing were essential modes of communication in this rural community and key to the success of the literacy programme, UPLIFT, which was developed by my collaborator Hizzaya Hissani based on the Freirean pedagogy of interactive participation and co-construction of knowledge (Freire, 1973). We recorded the women's communicative practices, at home and in the literacy programme, through observations, home visits, informal interviews, videotaped performances, and document collection. This reflection spotlights letter writing, secret role-play, and imagined literate identities.

All of the women in our study expressed personal reasons for wanting to learn to read and write, and correspondence through letters was of particular importance. Many wanted increased independence, including active participation in public events and the opportunity to connect with others who shared their interests. Their lack of experience with print and reading hindered participation in many public events because the women were either unable to read written announcements about such events or could not fully understand the participation requirements. Jane explained the problem this way: "I would like to know reading and writing because when they send for me a letter, or I receive a letter, somebody has to read for me instead of me reading for myself." She indicated that learning to read and write letters would help her "not be a cartoon" in her community, and she described the inherent challenges she faced when she had to travel on her own outside the familiarity of her village:

> There was a day I received a letter from Nebbi [town] telling me that I had to go to Nebbi for a workshop on Monday. I got the letter on Saturday. As I did not know how to read, I stayed with the letter, trying to look for someone to read it for me. My husband was not there, so I gave the letter to my brother-in-law to read for me. He looked at the letter and said, "Ee, you are being called for a job."
>
> "What kind of job?" I asked. "They said here 'workshop.' What does it mean?"
>
> The reader confidently replied, "It seems you are going to be a shopkeeper at Nebbi."
>
> "I don't think so," I replied. The reader did not know the meaning of the word workshop. Again, I had to look for someone else to read the letter for me. This time the reader told me the correct meaning. So on Sunday I prepared myself. On Monday my journey to Nebbi was also a problem because I did not know where Nebbi was and how I would know if I had reached it.

For the people in this rural community, letters were sent when important events such as a death or birth had taken place or when financial or family problems required attention. Letters were hand delivered from one community to another, carried by a community member travelling between different areas. Given the importance of letters, we were not surprised that many of the women placed such a high value on becoming independent. As Baynham (1995) reminds us, however, investigating literacy in social contexts involves understanding what people associate with literacy, how it is valued in particular communities, and how relations of power shape its use. In follow-up interviews, the women explained that being independent with their own letter reading and writing would enable them to (a) keep their own private affairs private, (b) avoid being "tricked" by someone who might relay false information when asked to read a letter, and (c) prevent marital problems by ensuring that they could act on orders sent by husbands when they were away from home. Each woman's reasons were deeply personal and strongly associated with her sense of self and her own literate identity in relation to inclusion and exclusion within her family and community.

In her study of the cycle of low literacy, Purcell-Gates (1995) illustrated that women who are unable to read and write live in another world, a world without print, and their exclusion and marginalization in their communities (and within their families) are primary factors in what she refers to as the status–literacy relationship. Similarly, in Zubair's (2004) study of Pakistani women's literacy practices, "illiterate" women refer to themselves as "silent birds" or "caged birds" (p. 87). For the women in our study, their perceptions of their own status as "illiterates" manifest in feelings of embarrassment, isolation, exclusion from community participation, and fear of losing their husbands. Jane's poignant reference to not wanting to be a "cartoon" provides a powerful image of a two-dimensional figure, something that is not fully human, an identity that, as Street (1994) points out, has long been associated with literacy in development contexts such as Uganda. Being "two-dimensional" was how many of the women in the literacy programme seemed to define themselves in relation to literacy and their status within their families and community. At the heart of their desire to read and write letters independently was the need to be recognized as active and contributing family and community members, and as such, to have the status and respect associated with a literate identity.

Participation in the literacy classes inspired many of the women to reconstruct their identities as literate beings. Two practices in particular caught my attention in relation to play and multimodality. First, several of the women labeled class materials such as writing tablets and books with their names in large letters, then placed these materials in clear plastic bags, and secured them in highly visible locations in their homes (e.g., above the door). Because most of their homes had few if any reading or writing materials, the presence of these labeled materials signaled to visitors that a literate person lived in that home. Second, some of the women adopted the practice of carrying pens and written materials whenever they were out in public. Letters were very important in this regard because of the limited availability of other kinds of print materials, such as books and newspapers. These "role-clothings" (e.g., props) (Sutton-Smith, 1959) similarly signaled to passers-by that they were in the presence of a literate woman. These literacy tools and materials served a critical purpose for the women; they allowed them to rehearse imagined "literate" identities as part of a special kind of secret role-play that enabled the women to test out at a distance how members of their community would respond to them as "literate" persons. The experience of being perceived as literate—if only in that fleeting moment of make-believe as they displayed their literacy materials and tools—allowed them to take on an imagined identity in an imagined community (Kanno & Norton, 2003) where they had an altered sense of belonging and being valued and where they could see themselves in the future as full participants in community events and activities such as political assemblies, workshops, and Bible study, independent of family or community literacy brokers.

Taking on this pretend identity in secrecy allowed the women to try on a role that they had not previously experienced or had reason to invest in. As adult learners engaged in make-believe role-play, they were able to mark themselves as different from many of the other women in their community. It permitted them an opportunity to alter ordinary life in which they were viewed as "illiterate" by the members of their community. This temporary suspension of normal life offered a new perspective as emerging members of the literacy club (Smith, 1987). The secret rehearsal of the role of "literate woman" performed within a kind of playground that became a temporary real world of its own whose effects were not lost when the role-play ended but rather continued as a kind of secret "radiance on the ordinary" (Huizinga, 1950/1955, p. 14) as a reason to invest in the rehearsed identity. Here, the women used role-play to create "an image of something different, something more beautiful, or more sublime" something different than who they were in everyday life. And by playing this role to such an extent that they lost consciousness of their ordinary reality, it became a realization in appearance, an imagined identity in an imagined community.

These imagined communities are situated at the intersection of play and multimodality; these play-based, imagined possibilities have considerable potential to influence the women's investment in learning how to read and write and present new possibilities for self, which can significantly influence the kinds of choices learners make about educational practices and may very well provide a reason and motivation for what they do in the present (Kanno & Norton, 2003). Indeed, as Kanno and Norton explain, "Our identities must be understood not only in terms of our investment in the 'real' world but also in terms of our investment in possible worlds" (p. 248) and in imagined worlds. For the women in this study, the opportunity to imagine themselves as literate members of their families and communities appears to be a strong factor in their motivation for wanting to succeed in the literacy programme. Because learners' visions of the future can be linked to their current actions and sense of self (Kanno & Norton, 2003), perhaps one of the most important benefits of participation in adult literacy programs is that it provides a space for learners to negotiate their own identities and an opportunity to imagine themselves as readers and writers long before they are able to read and write.

*****

In Chapter 1, I discussed play as foundational to synaesthetic activity in a young girl's multilingual literacy learning. In this chapter, I draw attention to the many ways in which imaginative play is integral to a range of multimodal practices, including digital and print based, understanding self and others, making sense of the past, and exploring the future. The examples in this chapter showcase the intimate connection between play and multimodality, a relationship that I have come to see as symbiotic in nature given the ways each system is beneficial to the other.

Historically, imaginative play has been integral to human development and culture (Huizinga, 1950/1955). With the unprecedented changes of the 21st century in terms of globalization and human communication, scholars need to reopen an interest in play via the detour of multimodality. The multimodal complexity of 21st-century communication requires the ability to put ourselves into the picture in ways we have not previously imagined.

Such interactive engagement involves risks and new skill sets and knowledge. Understanding the play element in this learning process in terms of its affordances and limitations may offer new ways forward in learning theories and pedagogical practices from early childhood to adulthood.

The examples in this chapter show how play offers unique opportunities for experimentation with different modes and communicative practices in a protected a space of learning whereby performance precedes competence (Cazden, 1981). Modes have different affordances and constraints. All learners "act out of a certain interest in the environment in which we are, and that in our making of signs, that interest is reflected in the sign in the best possible way, in the most plausible fashion, in the most apt form" (Kress, 1997, p. 19). These signs, including those constructed via play by the learners featured in this chapter, "show rationality, logic, human desire and affect" (Kress, 1997, p. 19). Play provides a unique and highly productive space for these individuals to select modes, identities, and narratives that suit their individual learning purposes and communicative needs and that enable them to reflect on their past, present, and future.

In their social semiotic account of designs for learning, Bezemer and Kress (2008) indicate that pedagogic interests need to respond to the question: "How can I best realize my preferred social relation with the imagined audience?" For the individuals featured in the four vignettes in this chapter, play offers a means to explore this question because it uniquely encapsulates multiple modes. When the limits of one mode are reached, a new mode seamlessly takes its place as the learner moves across and creates interactions among embodied language, gesture, and action. This synaesthetic, multimodal activity enables exploration of new identities and new audiences as modes are interwoven into stories. Connelly and Clandinin argue that stories "function as arguments in which we learn something essentially human by understanding an actual life or community as lived" (1990, p. 8). To return to points made at the outset of this chapter, there is an important relationship between the storyteller and intended audience, even when the most important audience is oneself, as in Geertz's notion of make-believe play as a story players tell themselves about themselves. As Holland and Lave have observed, "People [not just children] tell others who they are, but even more importantly, they tell themselves and then try to act as though they are who they say they are" (2001, p. 3).

In each of the imagined "stories" illustrated in this chapter, the learners showcase "something essentially human" as new understandings of their own lives or communities, whether real or imagined. Leticia's creation of a cumulative cultural text is an exploration of her family history and her own emerging identity as the child of refugee parents. The girls in the journalism club take on the role of journalist using role-clothings and modeling news reporters on TV within the liminal space of their after-school journalism club, imagining themselves as part of a professional community of journalists. Vincent remixes traditional storytelling with contemporary soccer news in his imagined identity as sportscaster, redefining what it means to be a brother in relation to his new responsibilities as caregiver. The women in the literacy programme take on the imagined identity of literate women as a means of investing in their own literacy learning, families, and communities. Each response represents a unique way of transforming the world according to what the individuals imagine in relation to their lived experience.

Without imaginative role-playing, these learners likely would not have the courage to rehearse and perform the new roles, skills, and tasks that are required of them in their new circumstances. In play, they are "a head taller" and a year more experienced in their knowledge of themselves, others, and the world around them. Performance in these play situations and scenarios takes place in different modes of thought, not just language, and as such, it enables problem solving and enhanced competence. It provides a tool for remembering and for carrying information from one learning context to another. The narrative thread in each of these examples and the central place of identity provides in the first example an opportunity for Leticia to walk around inside her parents' histories and experiences, and in the process to better understand her own identity as a young Canadian girl with a history that originates in China and Vietnam. In the second example, the multimodal tasks that journalists perform are first rehearsed in play—this helps the girls develop both the competence and the confidence to take on this role, complete with its range of multimodal tasks, in real world situations such as interviewing members of parliament and government officials. In the third example, Vincent performs for his brothers while simultaneously telling himself a story about himself, a story that uses humour and imagination to address the needs of his brothers and himself. In the final example, taking on an imagined literate identity enabled women to shift their status in the community. Imaginative role-playing provides critical and foundational learning in each of these examples.

Importantly, for each of the participants featured in the examples, play is a space where they can take on new identities that can be practiced and tested out through various modes. Engagement with these identities through imaginative role-play becomes a source for producing a continuous sense of who they are; this sense of self in the form of a continuous process becomes the means by which such identities can eventually come into existence (Bamberg & Georgakopoulou, 2008). These play texts are complex signs that represent "essentially human" situations and alternative perspectives and identities. Play as integral to learning and communication is all too often diminished, downplayed, or dismissed altogether, particularly in adolescent and adult learning contexts. In this chapter, the learners' ways of seeing and acting are nearly invisible yet second nature as the most apt way of meaning-making. Play with all of its multimodal possibilities enables "performance before competence" (Cazden, 1981) as identities are constructed and performed courageously. Research focusing on the symbiosis of play and multimodality can draw attention to the potentials and constraints of this relationship, to the agency of learners, and to the significance of play for learners of all ages.

NOTES

1. For an extended version of this example, see Kendrick (2003).
2. She is referring to all of the members of her extended family.
3. Wendy is the name of Leticia's pretend sister. It is also her cousin's name.
4. I am grateful to Margaret Early (University of British Columbia) and Walter Chemjor (Kabarak University) for their collaboration on this project. The extended study has been published in Kendrick, Chemjor, and Early (2012) and Kendrick, Early, and Chemjor (2013).
5. The larger study is published in Namazzi and Kendrick (2014).

REFERENCES

Bamberg, M., & Georgakopoulou, A. (2008). Small stories as a new perspective in narrative and identity analysis. *Text & Talk, 28*(3), 377–396.

Baynham, M. (1995). *Literacy practices: Investigating literacy in social contexts.* London, UK: Longman.

Bezemer, J., & Kress, G. (2008). Writing in multimodal texts: A social semiotic account of designs for learning. *Written Communication, 25*(2), 166–195.

Bruner, J. (1983). Play, thought, and language. *Peabody Journal of Education, 60*(3), 60–69.

Cazden, C. (1981). Performance before competence: Assistance to child discourse in the zone of proximal development. *Quarterly Newsletter of the Laboratory of Comparative Human Cognition, 3*(1), 5–8.

Connolly, F. M., & D. J. Clandinin (1990). Stories of experience and narrative inquiry. *Educational Researcher 19*(5), 2–14.

Dyson, A. H. (1997). *Writing superheroes: Contemporary childhood, popular culture, and classroom literacy.* New York, NY: Teachers College Press.

Finnegan, R. (2007). *The oral and beyond: Doing things with words in Africa.* Chicago, IL: University of Chicago Press.

Fiske, J. (1991). *Understanding popular culture.* Boston, MA: Unwin.

Freire, Paulo. *Pedagogy of the oppressed.* New York: Herder and Herder.

Gee, J. P. (2003). *What video games have to teach us about learning and literacy.* New York, NY: Palgrave/Macmillan.

Gee, J. P. (2005). Learning by design: Good video games as learning machines. *E-Learning, 2*(1), 5–16.

Geertz. C. (1973). *The interpretation of cultures.* New York: Basic Books.

Holland, D., Lachicotte, W., Jr., Skinner, D., & Cain, C. (1998). *Identity and agency in cultural worlds.* Cambridge, MA: Harvard University Press.

Holland, D. C., & Lave, J. (2001). *History in person: Enduring struggles, contentious practice, intimate identities.* Santa Fe, NM: School of American Research Press.

Huizinga, J. (1950/1955). *Homo Ludens: The study of the play element in culture.* Boston, MA: Beacon Press.

Kanno, Y., & Norton, B. (2003). Imagined communities and educational possibilities: Introduction. *Journal of Language, Identity, and Education,* 2(4), 241–249.

Kendrick, M. (2003). *Converging worlds: Play, literacy, and culture in early childhood.* Bern, Switzerland/New York, NY: Peter Lang.

Kendrick, M., Chemjor, W., & Early, M. (2012). ICTs as placed resources in a rural Kenyan secondary school journalism club. *Language & Education, 26*(4), 297–313.

Kendrick, M., Early, M., & Chemjor, W. (2013). Integrated literacies in a rural Kenyan girls' secondary school journalism club. *Research in the Teaching of English, 47*(4), 391–419.

Kendrick, M., & Hissani, H. (2007). Letters, literate identities, and imagined communities: Perspectives from rural Ugandan women. *Journal of Literacy Research, 39*(2), 195–216.

Kress, G. (1997). *Before writing: Rethinking the paths to literacy*. London, UK: Routledge.

Kress, G., & van Leeuwen, T. (1996). *Reading images: The grammar of visual design*. London, UK: Routledge.

Kress, G., & van Leeuwen, T. (2001). *Multimodal discourse: The modes and media of contemporary communication*. New York: Oxford Press.

Mitchell, C. (2014). Digital media and the knowledge-producing practices of young people in the age of AIDS. In K. Sanford, T. Rogers, & M. Kendrick (Eds.), *Everyday youth literacies* (pp. 81–93). Singapore, Malaysia: Springer.

Mushengyezi, A. (2003). Rethinking indigenous media: Rituals, "talking" drums and orality as forms of public communication in Uganda. *Journal of African Cultural Studies, 16*(1), 107–128.

Namazzi, E., & Kendrick, M. (2014). The use of multilingual cultural resources in child-headed households in Uganda. *Journal of Multilingual and Multicultural Development, 35*(7), 724–737.

Peek, P. M., & Yankah, K. (1994). The sounds of silence: Cross-world communication and the auditory arts in African societies. *American Ethnologist, 21*(3), 474–494. doi:10.1525/ae.1994.21.3.02a00020.

Purcell-Gates, V. (1995). *Other people's words: The cycle of low literacy*. Cambridge, MA: Harvard University Press.

Rowsell, J., & Pahl, K. (2007). Sedimented identities: Instances of practice. *Reading Research Quarterly, 42*(3), 388–404.

Smith, F. (1987). *Joining the literacy club: Further essays into education*. Portsmouth, NH: Heinemann.

Stein, P. (2008). Multimodal instructional practices. In J. Coiro, M. Knobel, C. Lankshear, & D. Leu (Eds.), *Handbook of research on new literacies* (pp. 871–898). New York, NY: Lawrence Erlbaum.

Street, B. (1994). Cross-cultural perspectives on literacy. In J. Maybin (Ed.), *Language and Literacy in Social Practice: A Reader* (pp. 139–150). Clevedon: Multilingual Matters.

Sutton-Smith, B. (1959). A formal analysis of game meaning. *Western Folklore, 18*(1), 13–24.

Vygotsky, L. (1978). *Mind in society: The development of higher psychological processes*. London, UK: Harvard University Press.

Weber, S., & Mitchell, C. (1995). *That's funny, you don't look like a teacher: Interrogating images of identity in popular culture*. London, UK: Falmer.

Zubair, S. (2004). Qualitative methods in researching women's literacy. In A. Robinson-Pant (Ed.), *Women, literacy, and development: Alternative perspectives* (pp. 85–99). London: Routledge.

3 Drawings as an Alternative Way of Understanding Young Children's Constructions of Literacy

Maureen Kendrick and Roberta McKay

When I first began to collect children's images of literacy at the turn of the 21st century (along with Roberta McKay), the landscape of literacy and communication in society was rapidly changing. In classrooms, however, the visual had little or no status, particularly in language and literacy education. At the time, literacy researchers were only just beginning to theorize the role of the visual in literacy practices, and analysis of visual communication in education was limited. This extended version of Kendrick and McKay (2004) reconsiders our initial findings in light of current language and literacy education policy, pedagogy, and practice. The purpose of this study, which built on our prior research and the method we developed (Kendrick, Anderson, Smythe, & McKay, 2003; Kendrick & McKay, 2003; Kendrick, McKay, & Moffatt, 2005; McKay & Kendrick, 2001a, b), was to investigate the ways in which the visual provides opportunities for young children from diverse backgrounds to communicate their literacy knowledge and experience.

We begin with the understanding that all students bring to the classroom knowledge that is constructed within the practices of their everyday lives outside of school, practices that integrate multiple modes of representation. The politics of how this knowledge is represented through various modes continues to raise challenges in classroom settings where learners and teachers come from diverse historical, sociocultural, and linguistic contexts (Stein, 2003). A major pedagogical challenge is to help children transform what they know into modes of representation that allow for a full range of human experience and to align approaches to language teaching, learning, and assessment with an individual child's strengths and styles of representation (Sidelnick & Svoboda, 2000). Although research demonstrates that children are able to communicate "powerful and imaginative ideas and problems" through a variety of symbol systems (Mitchell, 2011; Peterson, 1997; Weber & Mitchell, 1995; Wetton & McWhirter, 1998), in most instances, these alternative modes of representation remain undervalued in schools in general and in language and literacy education classes in particular (Stein, 2003; Zammit, 2011). Historically, narrow definitions of literacy, considerations for how knowledge is represented, and controversies around what counts as a legitimate text have been particularly problematic for students from diverse linguistic, cultural, and socioeconomic backgrounds (Zammit, 2011).

THE POLITICS OF REPRESENTATION IN LANGUAGE LEARNING

The cultural, economic, and social changes of the new century have meant that schools, colleges, and universities must determine how to deal with "new literate practices"; they must grapple with what it means to be a reader and writer in the 21st century (Luke & Elkins, 1998). According to Luke and Elkins,

> The most useful component of the toolkit for all literacy educators may not be the mastery of a particular method, but rather a vision of the future of literacy, a picture of the texts and discourses, skills and knowledge that might be needed by our students as they enter new worlds of work and citizenship, traditional and popular culture, leisure and consumption, teaching and learning.
>
> (1998, p. 4)

Literacy pedagogy must account for the rapidly increasing fusion of text forms embedded in children's lives by creating new opportunities for learners to communicate using multiple modes of representation in a variety of social contexts. Eisner (1985) and others (see, e.g., Cope & Kalantzis, 2009; New London Group, 1996) have argued that becoming literate means more than being able to read, write, or code; it means acquiring the ability to use a variety of representative forms for conceptualizing and expressing meaning. Kress and Jewitt (2003) emphasize that a multimodal approach to learning begins from the theoretical position of social semiotics, which treats all modes of meaning-making as equally significant.

Since the turn of the century, a growing number of literacy educators and researchers have been calling for a multiliteracies and multimodal approach to language learning that recognizes that meaning is made through multiple modes such as the visual, gestural, and audio, not just through language (Cope & Kalantzis, 2009; Kress, 2000, 2003; New London Group, 1996; Piazza, 1999). Their argument is that being multiliterate in today's society is a necessity rather than a luxury. The premise of a multiliteracies approach to literacy education is that meaning-making in classrooms will change to take into consideration the range of modes and ways in which students see themselves as literate, moving beyond the narrow focus on linguistic modes alone in mandated curriculums (Zammit, 2011). This broader definition of literacy goes beyond language symbols to that of multiple symbols. Critical to this perspective is the understanding that seniotic systems other than language are not "tack-ons" but rather relevant options for creating and expressing meaning. Mirzoeff asserts that the concept of visual culture is new because of the focus on the visual as a way of creating, expressing, and contesting meaning. He goes on to suggest that in Western culture, the spoken word consistently is elevated to the highest form of intellectual practice, and visual representations are considered merely "second-rate illustrations of ideas" (Mirzoeff, 1999, p. 6). As Kress argues, concepts explored in other modes are "every bit as demanding, rewarding, and significant as any concept expressed and explored in the medium of either spoken or written language" (1997, p. 21).

Our conceptual framework is also informed by Vygotsky's (1978) sociocultural theory. Of particular value is his premise that the transmission and acquisition of cultural knowledge such as literacy takes place on an interpersonal level between individuals before it is internalized on an intrapersonal level. An understanding of this recursive relationship between the individual and the culture enables us to view children's meaning construction as embedded in their social and cultural milieu. Further, Vygotsky's (1978) formulation of spontaneous concept development informs our analysis of the children's drawings. Spontaneous concepts develop from the child's personal experiences. While information obtained about children's literacy knowledge typically portrays literacy that is characterized by the conventional forms of practices and products found in schools (Barton, 1994), the images of literacy constructed by the children in their drawings provide us with insights into their "funds of knowledge" (Moll & Greenberg, 1990) and personal experiences of literacy, that is, what sense they have made of the complex world of literacy in their lives both inside and outside of school. Kress (2000) provides a strong argument for taking a completely fresh look at multimodality in theories of communication, and re-evaluating how we use different symbol systems to communicate and represent meaning. He stresses that it is critically important for this new agenda to include the full range of semiotic modes and a full understanding of their potentials and limitations. Central to this research is social semiotics, which attempts to explain and understand how signs are used to "produce and communicate meanings in specific social settings" (Kress & van Leeuwen, 1996, p. 264). Signs simultaneously communicate the here and now of a social context while representing the resources humans have "to hand" from the world around them (Kress, 1997).

Our focus in this chapter is on how young children communicate through the visual (i.e., drawing). Research consistently shows that drawing, as a means of investigating what children know, has "the potential to modify the dominant view of verbal knowledge as the primary representation of what average people know, and ultimately to advance knowledge of the role visual memory plays in human understandings of the world in which we live" (Peterson, 1997, p. 7). We recognize that there are dilemmas inherent in this expanded definition of literacy because as van Leeuwen (2015) notes, although multimodality has had a strong impact on educational theory and practice, many challenges remain in part because schools belong to a more formal and less multimodal period of development and, even in the 21st century, often fail to recognize the alternative modes of representing knowledge available in the culture.

METHOD AND ANALYSIS

Although an increasing number of educational researchers are using visual images such as drawings to investigate children's knowledge and understanding of particular topics and concepts (Mitchell, 2011; Peterson, 1997; Prosser, 1998; Weber & Mitchell, 1995; Wetton & McWhirter, 1998), our method for using children's drawings to understand their constructions of literacy is unique. We use a qualitative, interpretative research approach with a specific focus on image-based research (Kress & van Leeuwen, 1996; Mitchell, 2011; Prosser, 1998). It only has been within the last 30 years that qualitative researchers have given serious consideration to the use of images as a viable way of understanding aspects of humanity. Image-based research includes both moving forms such as films and videos and still images such as photographs, drawings, graffiti, and cartoons (see, e.g., Mitchell, 2011; Prosser, 1998). The images provide researchers with a different sequence of data and an alternative means of perceiving it. Specifically, the images are situated differently from other forms of data because visual images, in comparison with words, evoke for research participants a different way of viewing their own reality and a different way of understanding how they see themselves and how others see them. In other words, individuals see themselves reflected in images in a way they may not see themselves reflected in words. As Mitchell (2011) puts it, the visual provides learners with a mode of inquiry and representation as well as a mode of dissemination and engagement. From both a multimodal and a social constructivist stance, image-based research enables us to investigate the potential of drawing as an alternative way for children to make sense of, create, and represent themselves in relation to literacy.

This study is part of a larger study involving two elementary schools in a large urban city in western Canada. In this article, we focus on the Grade 1 and 2 (Primary 1 and 2) children because many of these children were just beginning to articulate their language and literacy experiences through school-assigned written language tasks, and we wanted to better understand how the visual offered an alternative to representing their knowledge and experience. Each data collection session, which lasted approximately 60 minutes, began with a class discussion about literacies in the children's lives, both inside and outside school. Our goal was to explore the children's images and ideas, so questions were used to guide the class discussions rather than rigidly format them. The directions for the drawing task, as outlined in Question 6, were deliberately left open-ended and did not specify who or what should be included in the drawing or where it might take place. The discussion provided the impetus for drawing, and we were aware that hearing the ideas of their peers could influence the children's drawing.

1. What kind of reading or writing do you do in school or outside of school?
2. Why do you read or write in school or outside of school?
3. Where do you read or write in school or outside of school?
4. How is reading or writing in school both similar and different from reading or writing outside of school?
5. How do you think you will use reading or writing in the future as you grow older?
6. Draw a picture of reading or writing. It can be a picture of reading or writing that you do at home or at school. It can be a picture of reading or writing that you do now or that you think you might do when you're older.

Following the group discussion and drawing session, the children met individually with one of the researchers or a research assistant to explain their drawings. The scribed or written explanations were used to verify the researchers' interpretations of the children's drawings (e.g., who and what was in the drawings, when and where the literacy event or activity took place, and why the children chose to draw what they did). Our overarching goal was to understand how the children represent literacy use in their everyday lives and to consider what these representations might mean for literacy pedagogy.

Our unit of analysis was the literacy practice or event portrayed in the drawing. Here, we draw on both Heath's (1983) and Street's (1984) conceptualizations, viewing literacy as "occasions in which written language is integral to the nature of participants' interactions and their interpretive processes and strategies" (Heath, 1983, p. 50) in relation to the social models of literacy that participants bring to bear upon those events and that give meaning to them (Street, 1984). The analysis involved coding the social settings and participants, reading and writing practices and genres, other modes of communication (e.g., speech, music, drama, and art), domains of practice (e.g., school, work, etc.), and social identities (e.g., reader, writer, teacher, and professional athlete) inherent in the literacy practice or event depicted. This information was then used to categorize each practice or event according to common themes and patterns. Both researchers worked together to code and analyse the data.

In the following sections, the predominant themes are presented along with brief examples of the range of literacy practices and events portrayed by these young children. Grade 1 largely comprised five-year-olds, and Grade 2 included mostly six-year-olds. In both schools, only children whose parents returned permission forms were included in the study. Pseudonyms are used throughout. Although descriptions of all the participating children's drawings are included in the analysis, we were only able to incorporate a select number of images.

Images of Literacy: Bolton Primary School

Bolton Primary was located in a middle to lower-middle socioeconomic neighbourhood. Like many Canadian schools, this school had a linguistically and culturally diverse student population. Home languages included Mandarin, Cantonese, Vietnamese, Croatian, Polish, Fijian, Acholi, and English, among others. The participants were 14 children in Grade 1 (10 girls and 4 boys) and 13 children in Grade 2 (8 girls and 5 boys).

Grade 1

Literacy in Home and Family Contexts

For this group of Grade 1 children, home and family contexts were the focal points of literacy. Of the 14 children, 10 portrayed literacy events that took place at home or with family members. The children who drew these pictures talked explicitly about reading with their mothers, sending messages and letters to relatives, and listening to stories read by older brothers and sisters. Their drawings reflect the children's knowledge of reading and writing for communication, maintaining family relationships, and one's own entertainment. Alex's portrayal of literacy involves his whole family; he drew a restaurant scene, which suggests that he is aware that dining out involves both reading (menus) and writing (recording food orders). However, unlike Alex, instead of portraying their entire family, many students included only siblings in their drawings. Robert's drawing, for instance, shows four figures; the one holding a book is his brother, and the three others represent Robert and his other two brothers; and he talked about his brother reading a story to him and the other two boys. Ainsley's drawing also includes siblings. It is a picture of her grandfather's house where she uses his computer with her brother and sister. Similar to Ainsley, Vina made reference to her siblings when she described the picture she drew of playing math games on the computer at home. These drawings capture snapshots of what Gregory (2001, p. 309) refers to as "synergy," "a unique reciprocity whereby siblings act as adjuvants in each other's learning." Gregory problematizes the view that in the majority of families, parents are the exclusive teachers of language and literacy. These drawings suggest that this group of children see their siblings as playing a more dominant role than their parents in their home literacy activities.

Maintaining emotional ties with absent family members, as an important motivation for literacy, was evident in other drawings. Brandy talked about writing a letter to her father, who did not live in the same household and worked for long periods outside the city. In her drawing, she included a pencil and a letter that reads, "Dear Dad How are you doing Love Brandy" (see Figure 3.1). On the reverse side, she drew her father and his written response to her letter: "Dear Brandy. I love you very much." The drawing done by Victoria was designed as a "book" for her mother. Inside the book, she wrote a poem. In discussing the drawing, she pointed out the hearts on

Figure 3.1 Brandy

the front cover and explained, "Now we're going into the middle. Let me read this to you: I like hearts. Hearts like me. I like me." Victoria's drawing also reflects her knowledge of the physical format of a book (front, middle, and back). In addition, her insistence on taking her drawing home that day to give to her mother is an indication of her strong sense of audience.

Other drawings that represent literacy events at home are those done by Ishrat, Samantha, and Katrina. Ishrat's representation of reading and writing is a picture of his house where he makes Lion King posters in the attic. In her drawing, Samantha provides an inventory of her bedroom in relation to reading and writing. Her drawing includes a book bag that contains the books she has read, a Valentine book that you can "make stuff out of," stickers for being good at day care, and a tray for holding papers. Katrina's drawing is one of the few that provides a window on her experience of school literacy. Her picture is an illustration of items she uses for playing school at home: a spelling test, a storybook from home, stickers, and check marks (see Figure 3.2). In her description of playing school, she made reference to "getting a happy face" for "getting the story right," getting tests and check marks, and earning certificates to go to McDonald's. Katrina's

Figure 3.2 Katrina

drawing characterizes school literacy as the rules and routines associated with story writing, test taking and home-reading programmes.

Imagined Literacies, Imagined Identities

Several of the children focused on how they might use literacy in the future, when they are older students or adults. Amy drew a "book about books" and explained, "When I grow up, I'm going to read a book about scary dinosaurs and tornadoes and about Valentine's and dogs" ' The cover of her book includes a dinosaur, a greeting card with a dog, two hearts, and a tornado, and the message: "I Love You Mom and DaD." Inside the book, Amy drew herself with a book in her hands, her name, and again included a dog, a tornado, and a Valentine heart. Her drawing reflects her knowledge of genre (information books and greeting cards), her reading preferences, and goals as a young reader. Kaela used both sides of a paper to illustrate reading and writing. On one side, she depicted herself and one of the researchers, and she talked about the fun they would have "doing reading and writing things" together. On the other side of the page, she again included herself along with two friends from day care. She explained that her picture is about books she is going to read someday at her day care, where they have "600 books." Shawn drew a scene from a Goosebumps book, a book his older brother can "kind of read," and a book that Shawn imagines reading in the future. Each of these drawings provides a vision of how these young children see themselves as readers in future contexts.

Grade 2

Literacy Across Different Social Settings and Domains

One of the most striking aspects of the ways in which the Grade 2 children in this school represented literacy was the broad array of settings and literacy events depicted in their drawings. The range included singing with the music teacher at her house, acting out *Romeo and Juliet* on a stage, working in an office building, and reading at school, at home, at the beach, and in a tent. This variety of settings and domains is reflective of the experiences this group of children have had with literacy both inside and outside school. Many of these literacy activities are extensions of the home domain.

Jodi's unique portrayal of literacy shows both music and writing as seniotic systems. In her drawing, she is sitting at a desk and holding a red-tipped pen. She clearly positions herself as a writer here. In front of the desk is Jodi's music teacher. Speech balloons indicate that Jodi is "doing the notes" and that her teacher is "singing the words" (see Figure 3.3). Ashley's illustration of the balcony scene from Shakespeare's *Romeo and Juliet*

Figure 3.3 Jodi

Figure 3.4 Ashley

communicates her understanding that a play is also an enactment of literacy (see Figure 3.4). She emphasized, “I like *Romeo and Juliet* because there’s all sorts of parts in there: There’s happy parts, and there’s sad parts, and there’s mad parts and stuff. I have drawn the part where Juliet is standing up by her bedroom door—and Romeo is down here saying, ‘Juliet!’ ” She then indicated that she has drawn hearts around Juliet’s head because “Romeo and Juliet are in love.” Her complex understanding of reading for aesthetic purposes is evident in the images her drawing evokes. Ashley’s experience with community theatre is quite extensive because she spends after-school time with her grandmother, who directs plays on a regular basis.

Kenny’s picture of the Capital City Tower provides a glimpse into his understanding of workplace literacy. His tower includes numerous windows behind which he has drawn offices with small figures working at computers. During our interview, he talked about visiting the Capital City Tower, where his father used to work. His perception of how reading and writing are used in this particular work environment was as follows: “They sit in their offices, and they typewrite the bill, and they write to the bank, and they have this little truck, and then they deliver it to whoever made it. This little truck goes to the bank, and then he hauls all the money out.” He also talked about his father being fired from his job in the office building and described how this affected his family, which could be an indication of why

Figure 3.5 Amber

the Capital City Tower was such a prominent image. Delacey described the beach, where she often spent time with her family, as a perfect place to "settle down and read." She drew herself standing on the beach with a book in hand: "It's a book about the beach," she explained, "stuff about sharks and fish." The blue sky and shining sun in her picture serve to create an atmosphere conducive to settling down to read.

Some of the Grade 2 children also drew literacy activities in or around their homes. Unlike the Grade 1 children, however, family members were not prominent figures in their drawings. Instead, they represented literacy events that included peers or that they did on their own. Amber, for instance, drew a colourful picture of a large, red tent with three small figures sitting and reading in front of it (see Figure 3.5). She explained, "I like to make tents in my bedroom and read with a flashlight." This is a favourite activity to do with friends who spend the night.

Michael's representation of literacy also relates to home. He drew his father's house, which is where he spends weekends, and explained that at his father's house, he plays games with his cousin and his step-cousin. Michael's drawing also has the added feature of the caption "On the Weekend, I go With My Dad and Mom." The drawing resembles a typical page in a journal diary (see Figure 3.6). It is unclear from Michael's drawing and his description whether his intention was to illustrate playing games as a reading and writing activity or whether the journal-type page he produced was his image of writing.

Figure 3.6 Michael

Ashley D. portrayed herself reading a book at her desk with her cat watching. Although she described the desk as a place where she likes to sit and read, she explained that usually the seat is where her older brother chooses to sit. Kimberly's drawing represents her favourite place for reading and writing, which is the front step of her house, where she likes to do her math homework and read. Viannara's drawing also represents a favourite reading spot, which she described as "the table between the living room and the kitchen." She explained that this was where she read *The Ugly Duckling*. Brian's drawing illustrates his reading spot at school—at his desk.

Imagined Literacies, Imagined Identities

Jocelyn's portrayal of literacy moves beyond the here and now into a place where she imagines reading and writing taking place. Her picture is of a large building. "When I think about reading and writing, it sounds like you need a big place for that," she explained. Jocelyn went on to talk about her understanding of the writing process as it would take place in this imaginary building: "One person might be writing about penguins, or someone might be writing about health, or someone might be reading. Someone might be the person who reads all the book to see if it's good. [If the book is good], they put it in the library. [If the book is bad], the person who writed the story. It doesn't sound good. There has to be a solution and problem and where it takes place and the characters. And something has to be at the end, that they lived happily ever after. So then they might have to make a different story." Jocelyn's description of her drawing represents a remarkable understanding of genre, text structures, and book publishing.

Jackson Primary School

Jackson Primary School was in a middle to upper-middle socioeconomic neighbourhood. In total, 19 students in Grade 1 (7 girls and 12 boys) and 21 students in Grade 2 (13 girls and 8 boys) participated in the study. Similar to Bolton Primary, this school had a diverse population of students whose home languages included Mandarin, Cantonese, Croatian, Ukrainian, and English, among others.

Grade 1

Literacy in Home and Family Contexts

Of the 19 children in this classroom, 14 represented literacy events at home or in other contexts with their families, which was also the most frequently depicted literacy setting in the drawings of the Bolton Grade 1 students. Illustrations of favourite reading places at home were very common. Taylor, for example, drew a picture of himself sitting on what looks like a very comfortable couch reading "Weany the Poo" (see Figure 3.7). The reading event

Figure 3.7 Taylor

is encapsulated in a cloud, which vividly illustrates the experience of reading as separate from the here and now. The image communicates the experiential aspect of being completely absorbed in reading much more lucidly than language. Cole's colourful picture of reading Pokémon (a television cartoon character) in his bedroom reflects his reading preferences at home. Other examples that portray literacy at home include Taylor's picture of herself reading in her basement and Logan's drawing of the bookshelf in his bedroom. Catrina also shows herself at home in her room, a place where she has many tools for literacy, namely books on a shelf and a special desk for reading and writing. Jordan drew an amusing picture of what often happens when he is reading books in his room at night: "I was sleeping [because] I couldn't read any more books" (see Figure 3.8). Alternatively, T. J. depicts his mother rather than himself as a reader. His picture shows her reading a book in the house, while he is playing outside.

Brett's picture is also set in a home context; in the picture, he is reading his favourite fairy tales and doing math homework. The picture shows an active engagement in the reading process and provides examples of both home and school literacies. Other children also included both home and

Figure 3.8 Jordan

school literacies in their illustrations. Sebastian, for example, drew a picture of getting a book from the school library to read to his mom and dad at home. Tyler, like Brett, drew a picture of doing math homework, and from the smile drawn on his face. one can infer it is something he enjoys.

Imagined Literacies, Imagined Identities

Four of the students in the Grade 1 class took from the whole-class discussion the idea of how they might use literacy in the future when they are adults. Kathleen imagined herself in the future teaching ABCs to kindergarten children. Melody saw herself as a soccer coach: her picture shows her studying a book about coaching. Jaleesa depicted herself as a camp counsellor reading a book to children around a campfire. Zack, who dreams of becoming a professional hockey player for the Edmonton Oilers, illustrated an autograph signing session (see Figure 3.9). Interestingly, it was primarily girls who imagined themselves in future roles; many of these roles involved

Figure 3.9 Zack

teaching literacy to children in one capacity or another. In comparison, Zack most likely viewed literacy as a tangential skill for someone who plays hockey.

Metalinguistic Awareness

Young readers and writers, when given the opportunity, frequently demonstrate metalinguistic awareness, including not only knowledge about the structures of language but also "beliefs about oneself and others as language users, knowledge about the demands of different literacy events, a repertoire of language strategies, and knowledge about orchestrating this complex of concepts and strategies in the face of particular literacy events" (Rowe & Harste, 1986, p. 236). Unique to this group of children is that two of them demonstrated through the visual an awareness of what takes place inside a writer's head during the writing process. Jesse uses thought balloons to indicate what he and his friend are thinking about while they write stories at school. Dylan's drawing represents what he imagines while writing a story about dinosaurs.

Grade 2

Literacy in Home and Family Contexts

Like many other children in this study, this group of Grade 2 children frequently represented literacy in home and family domains. In total, 9 of the 21 children portrayed literacy events at home or with family members. Devyn's picture of his mother reading in bed (see Figure 3.10) provides a snapshot of a literacy event in his household. The drawing reveals his familiarity with the event and the type of books his mother likes to read. Esther's picture is also a portrayal of a common literacy event in many homes—doing homework at the kitchen table. Equally representative of household literacy is Matthew's drawing of himself reading books while simultaneously watching television. Nicola depicts two roles in her drawing: the first as a student doing a spelling test at the kitchen table with her mother, the second as an artist.

A variation in how these children portrayed home literacy events, however, is the increased inclusion of technology in their drawings. In total, four of the nine children who represented home and family literacy events drew pictures that related to the use of computers at home. Mitchel drew himself using a computer to write a Cinderella story. His drawing represents both an awareness of genre and his knowledge of computers as word processors. Chantelle depicted herself using the computer to write a story about her cat. Two other children also included computers in their drawings. Brent drew a picture of his friend Kelsey playing a game on his computer at home. Katie, who does not yet have a computer, drew a picture of the computer she is "going to get."

An extension of home and family literacy is the inclusion of literacy events with friends in home contexts. Kelsey's drawing is an illustration of her friend Shelby writing a story. The caption for her drawing is: "This is Shelby writing lots. It

Figure 3.10 Devyn

is at her house. She has lots of books." Shelby similarly depicted reading and writing with Kelsey, pointing out that Kelsey is sitting beside her in the picture she has drawn. Dyson (1993) uses the term "social work" to refer to the role writing can play in defining and bonding friendships in a classroom. In the case of Shelby and Kelsey, drawing appears to serve an identical purpose to writing. For these young girls, inserting each other into their drawings defines, confirms, and perhaps maintains their friendship in the classroom.

Imagined Literacies, Imagined Identities

Several of the students in this class depicted how they imagined themselves as readers and writers in the future. Brandon, for instance, portrayed himself as a soccer player. Similar to Zack, the Grade 1 student who dreamed

Figure 3.11 Meyna

of becoming a hockey player, Brandon pictured himself in the prestigious role of a professional athlete who is frequently asked to sign autographs for the public. Meyna saw her future role as a teacher. In her drawing, she is "teaching about science—how the stars grow and shine" (see Figure 3.11). Kara imagined being a tap dancer, and she drew a picture of herself reading a book that would help her accomplish this goal. Sabrina's drawing is also about the future, but rather than depicting a particular role, she drew pictures of books, complete with titles (*The kings little girl*, *Baby truble*, and *The frog prince*) that she would like to read in the future. Ursula's picture is of an imaginary scene at the public library. Her description of the drawing reveals her awareness that books can evoke a range of responses in readers: "These are kids reading books. The boy is surprised with his book. The girl is happy with hers. These children are at the public library." Deanna's very colourful and abstract picture is also of the public library, a place where she imagines there are "280 books" (see Figure 3.12). "I've never been to a public library," she wrote, "but maybe I probably will."

Literacy in School and Community Contexts

With the exception of the drawings described in this section, there are very few examples of children positioning themselves as students in classrooms or depicting examples of school literacy events. Zeina drew a picture of

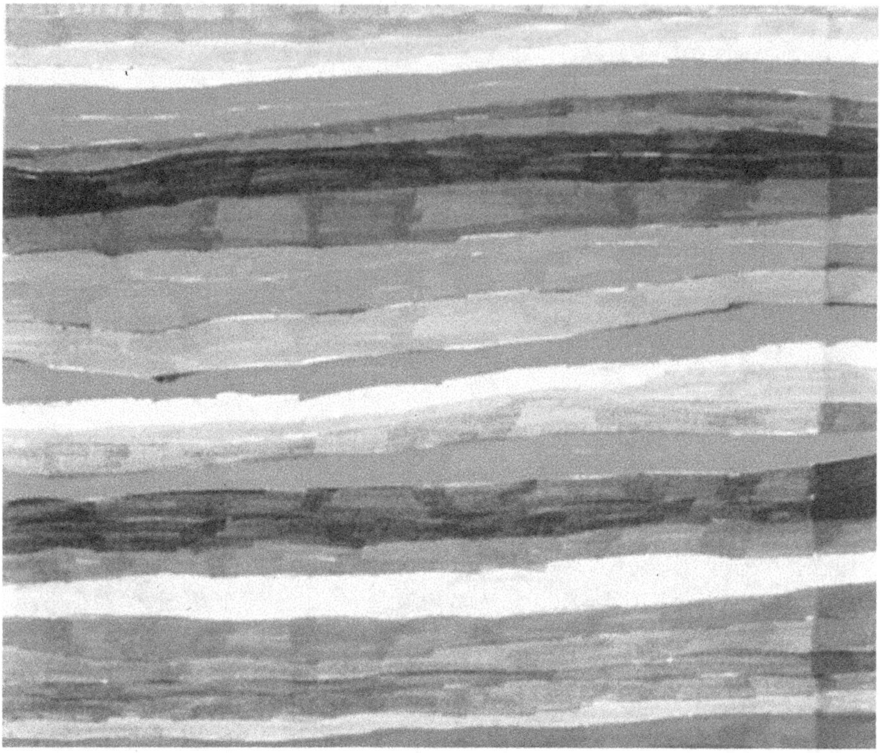

Figure 3.12 Deanna

her own classroom and portrayed her teacher "teaching math" and "reading to the kids." When writing about her drawing, she provided a detailed description of the classroom organization: "There is a brown table beside the orange one. There is a door right beside the brown table. There is a chalkboard and the places where you put the chalk. The erasers go on the chalk thing." Garratt's picture shows him reading at school with the caption: "When I was in [Grade] 2." The smile drawn on his face suggests a positive attitude. Both Nathan and John inserted themselves into their drawings. Nathan pictured himself reading his journal at school and wrote the following descriptive caption: "I have a game boy. I have a play station." Similarly, John drew an aerial view of the top of his desk, with a piece of writing positioned in the centre, and wrote this caption: "I like my game boy and I like playing it. I got a new fire pit and I have firinit [fire in it]." The writings that these two students integrated into their drawings reveal something about who they are in out-of-school contexts. The captions also suggest that, like many five- and six-year-old boys, both boys have a preference for what Newkirk (2000) refers to as "visually mediated narratives." such as video games and computer graphics.

DRAWING AS AN ALTERNATIVE MODE OF REPRESENTATION IN LANGUAGE LEARNING

In the discussion that follows, we return to the politics of representation in language learning, which was highlighted poignantly for us when we shared the students' drawings with their classroom teachers. Although our young participants were instinctively operating within a multiliteracies framework, their teachers were not. The teachers overwhelmingly were surprised that their students were able to express complex understandings of reading and writing, which apparently were not evident in classroom language arts activities. Their responses emphasize the privileged position that language holds over other forms of representation in many classrooms. Unlike language-dependent modes of representation, the drawings allow these young children to represent whole areas of their sensory lives. Like snapshots, the pictures capture sensory modes such as sight, smell, hearing, taste, and touch in a way that language cannot; they infer the moods, sentiments, relationships, and interactions that are embedded and diffused across the many different literacy contexts of children's lives. Kress (2000) points out that "the general assumption is that language is a communicational and representational medium which is fully adequate to the expression of anything that we might want to express: that anything that we think, feel, sense, can be said (or written) in language" (p. 193). This assumption places language in an exceptionally privileged position, particularly in early childhood classrooms, where many young children are just learning to use print to represent their understanding of the world.

The human mind, Hubbard (1989) posits, has a need for organizational systems that sort out the kaleidoscope of images to which we are exposed. Both art and language provide a means of encoding experience, whether real or imagined (Baron, 1984). However, as Kress argues, the two modes—art and language—are "embedded in distinct ways of conceptualising, thinking, and communicating" (Kress, 2000, p. 195). Drawings, he explains, show an astonishing conceptual understanding and imagination that cannot be expressed through language, even language in narrative format.

The basis of this study is that children's drawings about reading and writing have unrealized potential for understanding how they use alternative seniotic systems to make sense of the literacies in their lives. Drawings are children's earliest representations of experience and stimulate their narrative impulse to create stories (Vygotsky, 1978). According to Sidelnick and Svoboda (2000, p. 174), "aesthetic, narrative, and reflective inquiries using the arts help children attain new conceptual language to organize and express their learning, and serve as an instrument for acquiring knowledge." This collection of drawings demonstrates that young children's visual representations of their own literacy can provide teachers and researchers with additional or alternative ways of understanding children's constructions of reading and writing, including their metalinguistic awareness. Interestingly, van Leeuwen (2015) points out, that as a student of linguistics, he was told that only language is capable of "metalanguage," language to talk about language. Dyson (1992) and Sidelnick and Svoboda (2000) point out, drawing also can act as a bridge from one symbol system to another, in this case, from image to word. In addition, print literacy can be made more appealing and accessible when it is embedded in systems that are more attractive to the learner. As Newkirk (2000, p. 297) observes, "primary-school children regularly break into print by making elaborate drawings with a label at the bottom—print literacy being pulled in the wake of the visual."

Interacting through different communicative forms carries with it assertions—tacit or conscious—"about the kind of person one (and other) is, how one is (currently being) related to others, and what feelings are to be associated with the social arrangement" (Carbaugh, 1999, p. 160). In learning language, and learning through the use of that language, children move in and out of different social contexts, and by engaging in the practices specific to these contexts, they come to understand how to position themselves as people with recognizable social identities. Dillon and Moje (1998, p. 194) use the phrase "occupying subject positionings" to emphasize that these positionings are "temporary, fluid, and context dependent." Positionings, in other words, are possible ways of being and each person's experience of those possibilities as they are made available through specific discourses and contexts (Fernie, Davies, Kantor, & McMurray, 1993).

In occupying subject positionings, children necessarily become involved in positioning themselves as gendered beings (Davies, 1989). Cherland (1994) reminds us that gender is not something people are, but rather, it is something people do. The young children in this study have learned to "perform" gender, as Barrs (2000) observes, by taking on roles and playing with and being curious about not only the roles but also the idea of themselves in those roles. The drawings are a performance of imagined future gendered identities that are inextricably linked to imagined literacies that transcend time and space. In the here and now of their drawings, these children are teachers, sports heroes, readers, writers, and friends who engage in literate practices that allow them to enact how they position themselves as boys and girls or men and women.

The visual for these children gives shape to their interests, purposes, and intentions as meaning-makers. The various examples of literacy events and practices they portray represent their different ways of taking meaning from the environment (Heath, 1982). Their drawings show us the situated literacies in their everyday lives, the features of which schools can potentially draw upon. Each drawing serves to raise questions about what counts as literacy for these children; the depicted literacies involve much more than actions with texts; they "connect to, and are shaped by, values, attitudes, feelings, and social relationships" (Perry, 2012, p. 54).

*****

The children in this study produced unique texts into which their personal and social histories were woven. By using what they "have to hand," children make their own representational resources part of a constant production of signs (Kress & van Leeuwen, 1996). The interests of the sign-makers lead them to select what they want to represent in a particular moment and context and determine the process. Through drawing about reading and writing, young children are able to transform what they know about print into a mode of representation that allows for the full range of their experience. As researchers, the drawings give us a glimpse into the "spontaneous concepts" being developed by the children in relation to literacy in their lives, both inside and outside of school. Their drawings communicate the diverse ways in which they see themselves and others as literate beings; these identity displays are still in the making or just coming into being. In addition, they also showcase their wealth of literacy experiences across contexts such as home, school, and community, which demonstrate their keen awareness that literacy tools (e.g., books, pencils, paper, and computers) are used in different ways in different communities of practice (Anning, 2003). As we move from a culture dominated by language to one in which images are becoming increasingly important (Cope & Kalantzis, 2009; Kress & van Leeuwen, 1996; New London Group, 1996), it is critical that current literacy policy debates include broader aspects of communication beyond "lettered representation" (Bearne & Kress, 2001). Yet, in revisiting the original multiliteracies manifesto, Cope and Kalantzis (2009) comment that in literacy education, "not much has changed in the years since we first wrote [1996]. The two sides of the political spectrum, remain poles apart in what they see as the appropriate role of literacy learning in society, and indeed, education in general" (p. 167). At the core of current literacy development paradigms in many global contexts remain the literate behaviours traditionally associated with learning to decode and encode print (Anning, 2003) and which continue to place the linguistic mode in an exceptionally privileged position.

On the whole, the visual aspects of early literacy in particular and graphical forms of representation in general remain "under-valued, under-researched, and under-represented," and within institutional settings, young children's meaning-making unremittingly is still geared toward narrow definitions of literacy and numeracy (Anning, 2003, p. 5). What is now required more than ever are educational innovations that focus more on the heuristics of learners discovering the possibilities afforded by visual and other modes (Cope & Kalantzis, 2009). A second prong of this argument is made by van Leeuwen (2015), who stresses that, "having studied modes in general, we should now turn our attention to the specific visual literacies of school subjects and domains of institutional practice, and seek to ensure that these form part of teacher education at a high level" (pp. 587–588). We see collecting young children's images of literacy as a starting point for such an agenda, not only in terms of providing teachers a window on their students' situated literacy lives and funds of knowledge but also in terms of their own understanding of the potential and possibilities of the visual. Integral to such an agenda, however, is the need to focus more on the role of the visual in communicative practices more broadly rather than continuing to frame studies of the visual simply on the need to understand literacy (Yamada-Rice, 2015).

REFERENCES

Anning, A. (2003). Pathways to the graphicacy club: The crossroad of home and pre-school. *Journal of Early Childhood Literacy, 3*(1), 5–35.

Baron, N. S. (1984). Speech, sight, and signs: The role of iconicity in language and art. *Semiotica, 52*(3/4), 187–211.

Barrs, M. (2000). Gendered literacy? *Language Arts, 77*(4), 287–293.

Barton, D. (1994). *Literacy: An introduction to the ecology of written language.* Cambridge, MA: Blackwell.

Bearne, E., & Kress, G. (2001). Editorial. *Reading, Literacy and Language, 35*(3), 89–93.

Carbaugh, D. (1999). Positioning as display of cultural identity. In R. Harré & L. van Langenhove (Eds.), *Positioning theory: Moral contexts at intentional action* (pp. 160–177). Oxford, UK: Blackwell.

Cherland, M. R. (1994). *Private practices: Girls reading fiction and constructing identity.* Bristol, PA: Taylor & Francis.

Cope, B., & Kalantzis, M. (2009). "Multiliteracies": New literacies, new learning. *Pedagogies: An International Journal, 4*(3), 164–195.

Davies, B. (1989). The discursive production of the male/female dualism in school settings. *Oxford Review of Education, 15*(3), 229–241.

Dillon, D., & Moje, E. (1998). Listening to the talk of adolescent girls: Lessons about literacy, school, and life. In D. Alvermann, K. Hinchman, D. Moore, S. Phelps & D. Waff (Eds.), *Reconceptualizing the literacies in adolescents' lives* (pp. 193–223). Mahwah, NJ: Lawrence Erlbaum Associates.

Dyson, A. H. (1992). The emergence of visible language: Interrelationships between drawing and early writing. *Visible Language, 16*(4), 360–381.

Dyson, A. H. (1993). *The social world of children learning to write in an urban primary school.* New York, NY: Teachers College Press.

Eisner, E. W. (1985). *The art of educational evaluation: A personal view.* London, UK: Falmer Press.

Fernie, D. E., Davies, B., Kantor, R., & McMurray, P. (1993). Becoming a person in the preschool: Creating integrated gender, school culture, and peer culture positionings. *Qualitative Studies in Education, 6*(2), 95–110.

Gregory, E. (2001). Sisters and brothers as language and literacy teachers: Synergy between siblings playing and working together. *Journal of Early Childhood Literacy, 1*(3), 301–322.

Heath, S. B. (1982). What no bedtime story means: Narrative skills at home and school. *Language in Society, 11*, 49–76.

Heath, S. B. (1983). *Ways with words: Language, life, and work in communities and classroom.* Cambridge: Cambridge University Press.

Hubbard, R. (1989). *Authors of pictures, draughtsmen of words.* Portsmouth, NH: Heinemann.

Kendrick, M. (2015). The affordances and challenges of visual methodologies in literacy studies. In J. Rowsell & K. Pahl, *The Routledge Handbook of Literacy Studies* (pp. 619–633). New York, NY: Routledge.

Kendrick, M., Anderson, J., Smythe, S., & McKay, R. (2003). What images of family literacy reveal about family literacy practices and family literacy programs. In C. Fairbanks, J. Worthy, B. Maloch, J. Hoffman & D. Schallert (Eds.), *52nd yearbook of the National Reading Conference* (pp. 245–271). Oak Creek, WI: National Reading Conference, Inc.

Kendrick, M., & McKay, R. A. (2003). Revisiting children's images of literacy. *Language & Literacy, 5*(1). Retrieved from: http://educ.queensu.ca/~landl/index.htm

Kendrick, M., & McKay, R. (2004). Drawings as an alternative way of understanding young children's constructions of literacy. Journal of Early Childhood Literacy, 4(1), 109–128.

Kendrick, M., McKay, R., & Moffatt, L. (2005). The performance of self in children's drawings of home, school and community literacies. In J. Anderson, M. Kendrick, T. Rogers, & S. Smythe (Eds.), *Portraits of literacy across families, communities, and schools: Intersections and tensions* (pp. 185–204). Mahwah, NJ: Lawrence Erlbaum.

Kress, G. (1997). *Before writing: Rethinking the paths to literacy.* London, UK: Routledge.

Kress, G. (2000). Multimodality. In B. Cope & M. Kalantzis (Eds.), *Multiliteracies: Literacy learning and the design of social futures* (pp. 182–202). London, UK: Routledge.

Kress, G. (2003). *Literacy in the new media age.* London, UK: Routledge.

Kress, G., & Jewitt, C. (2003). Introduction. In C. Jewitt & G. Kress (Eds.), *Multimodal literacy* (pp. 1–18). New York, NY: Peter Lang.

Kress, G., & van Leeuwen, T. (1996). *Reading images: The grammar of visual design.* London, UK: Routledge.

Luke, A., & Elkins, J. (1998). Reinventing literacy in "New Times." *Journal of Adolescent and Adult Literacy, 42*(1), 4–8.

McKay, R., & Kendrick, M. (2001a). Children draw their images of reading and writing. *Language Arts, 78*(6), 529–533.

McKay, R., & Kendrick, M. (2001b). Images of literacy: Young children's drawings about reading and writing. *Canadian Journal of Research in Early Childhood Education, 8*(4), 7–22.

Mirzoeff, N. (1999). *An introduction to visual culture.* London, UK: Routledge.

Mitchell, C. (2011). *Doing visual research.* London, UK: Sage.

Moll, L., & Greenberg, J. (1990). Creating zones of possibilities: Combining social contexts for instructions. In L. Moll (Ed.), *Vygotsky and education* (pp. 319–348). Cambridge, UK: Cambridge University Press.

Newkirk, T. (2000). Misreading masculinity: Speculations on the great gender gap in writing. *Language Arts, 77*(4), 294–300.

New London Group. (1996). A pedagogy of multiliteracies: Designing social futures. *Harvard Educational Review, 66*(1), 60–92.

Perry, K. (2012). What is literacy? A critical overview of sociocultural perspectives. *Journal of Language and Literacy Education, 8*(1), 50–71.

Peterson, R. W. (1997). Visual memory and language: A study of children's use of art and language to communicate their knowledge of science. Paper presented at the annual meeting of the National Association for Research in Science Teaching, Oak Brooks, IL.

Piazza, C. L. (1999). *Multiple forms of literacy: Teaching literacy and the arts.* Upper Saddle River, NJ: Prentice-Hall.

Prosser, J. (1998). *Image-based research.* London, UK: Falmer Press.

Rowe, D., & Harste, J. (1986). Metalinguistic awareness in writing and reading: The young child as curricular informant. In D. Yaden & S. Templeton (Eds.), *Metalinguistic awareness and beginning literacy: Conceptualizing what it means to read and write* (pp. 235–256). Portsmouth, NH: Heinemann.

Sidelnick, M. A., & Svoboda, M. L. (2000). The bridge between drawing and writing: Hannah's story. *The Reading Teacher, 54*(2), 174–184.

Stein, P. (2003). Representation, rights, and resources: Multimodal pedagogies in the language and literacy classroom. In B. Norton & K. Toohey (Eds.), *Critical pedagogies and language learning* (pp. 95–115). Cambridge, UK: Cambridge University Press.

Street, B. (1984). *Literacy in theory and practice*. Cambridge: Cambridge University Press.

van Leeuwen, T. (2015). Multimodality in education: Some directions and some questions. *TESOL Quarterly*, *49*(3), 582–589.

Vygotsky, L. (1978). *Mind in society: The development of higher psychological processes*. Cambridge, MA: Harvard University Press.

Weber, S., & Mitchell, C. (1995). *That's funny, you don't look like a teacher*. London, UK: Falmer Press.

Wetton, N., & McWhirter, J. (1998). Images and curriculum development in health education. In J. Prosser (Ed.), *Image-based research* (pp. 263–283). London, UK: Falmer Press.

Yamada-Rice, D. (2015). Cultural affordances of visual mode texts in and of Japanese landscapes and young children's emerging comprehension of semiotic texts. In J. Rowsell & K. Pahl (Eds.), *The Routledge handbook of literacy studies* (pp. 308–321). London, UK: Routledge.

Zammit, K. P. (2011). Connecting multiliteracies and engagement of students from low socio-economic backgrounds: Using Bernstein's pedagogic discourse as bridge. *Language and Education*, *25*(3), 203–220.

4 The Affordances and Challenges of Visual Methodologies in Literacy Studies[1]

In this chapter, I argue that the increasingly complex nature of literacy in the 21st century requires rethinking current literacy research methodologies. I make a case for using visual methodologies and multimodal ethnography to gain access to the accretive layers of literacy practices in the everyday worlds of individuals, families, and communities. I use visual examples taken from collaborative literacy as social practice research that brings together ethnographic methods with multimodality in a series of studies that I have conducted in Uganda over the past 10 years. Taken together, the vignettes demonstrate the potential of visual methodologies for accessing the emic in literacy studies in a range of contexts. The vignettes unravel some of the different constructs, issues, and emerging questions associated with studying literacy in diverse community settings, opening broader dialogues on literacy that move beyond more traditional methods of data collection and analysis.

HISTORICAL PERSPECTIVE

There is a considerable body of interdisciplinary research investigating the nature of literacy yet with little agreement on the topic. My collaborative research draws broadly from the fields of linguistics, anthropology, ethnographies of communication, and sociology with a focus on the increasing recognition that literacy is not only a skill to be learned but a practice that is socially constructed and locally negotiated (see, e.g., Baynham, 1995; Fairclough, 1992; Heath, 1983; New London Group, 1996). The research studies described in this chapter use a New Literacy Studies framework, which considers literacy as multiple and varied according to time and place but also contested in relations of power (Street, 1984). Baynham (1995) argues that investigating literacy from this perspective involves documenting not only the visible aspects of what people do with literacy but also the *invisible* aspects of literacy: namely, the values, associations, ideologies, and power relationships that surround literacy in a particular community. Carrington likewise argues for a critical view whereby literacy is conceptualized as providing skills and knowledge to mediate self in relation to one's social and cultural context. She emphasizes, "literacy is about who you are allowed to become in a given society" (2003, p. 96).

The different ways we use, value, and think about literacy and its material and cultural resources constitute the accretive layers that researchers and educators seek to uncover and make sense of in literacy studies. These differences place emphasis on the situatedness of literacy, what Street (1984) refers to as an "ideological model" (as opposed to an autonomous one). Literacy researchers working within an NLS tradition have documented and theorized literacy's cultural and communicative resources in a variety of ways, including multiple modes (Kress, 2000; Pahl, 2003), syncretic literacies (Gregory, 1998, 2001), "funds of knowledge" (Moll, Amanti, Neff, & Gonzàlez, 2005), "local literacies" (Barton & Hamilton, 1998), cultural and mediational tools (Hull & Katz, 2006), and "linguistic resources" (de la Piedra, 2006). These diverse resources are grounded in the material and social conditions in which individuals live and work; their modes of learning and participating in social, spiritual, and cultural events; their health and healing practices; and their child-rearing practices (Smythe & Toohey, 2009).

The research I report on focuses on the visual as a communicative and cultural resource within the context of Uganda. The work blends multimodality and ethnography with other theories and methods to gain access to the invisible aspects of literacy practices in diverse communities. Although the use of visual data has a long history in disciplines such as visual anthropology (see, e.g., Banks & Morphy, 1997), such data has received far less attention in other disciplines, including literacy studies (Hamilton, 2000). Some exceptions include Hamilton (2000), Heath (see, e.g., Heath & Wollach, 2007), Hodge and Jones (1996), and Mannion and Ivanic (2007).

CRITICAL ISSUES AND TOPICS

Literacy research recently has seen a more widespread engagement with the diversity of modes used in meaning-making (e.g., visual, auditory, and embodied). Dicks, Flewitt, Lancaster, and Pahl (2011) speculate that this increasing engagement has been spurred on by "the new forms of communication that have emerged in a digitally negotiated world, and by the ready accessibility of visual methods for documenting social interaction"; the trend "points both to the study of meaning (semiotics) and of social context (ethnography)" (2011, p. 229). According to Kress and van Leeuwen (1996), social semiotics seeks to explain and understand how signs are used to produce and communicate meanings across social settings. Signs such as visual images are instances of social context and represent the various resources available to individuals within their specific settings (Kress, 1997; Vygotsky, 1978). The meanings encoded in these visual representations are also a reflection of the sign-maker's reality as they imagine it and as influenced by what they believe and value. This multimodal and social semiotic perspective recently has been merged with ethnography in literacy studies, the vast majority of which have taken place in North America, western Europe, and Australia. There is currently a dearth of similar research on literacy practices in economically under-resourced contexts such as sub-Saharan Africa.

My own literacy research in East Africa seeks to broaden this perspective (see, e.g., Kendrick & Jones, 2008; Kendrick, Early, & Chemjor, 2013; Kendrick, Jones, Mutonyi, & Norton, 2009; Kendrick & Mutonyi, 2007). The three "telling" examples that I include in this chapter focus exclusively on the visual, a mode that has been foregrounded in much of the theorizing in multimodality (e.g., Kress's seminal work in particular). Over the past decade, my experience as a literacy researcher working with visual images produced in Uganda in particular has raised two key issues associated with multimodal and visual ethnographic research: the limitations of methods available for critically analysing images produced in non-Western communities and the need to more fully consider context, particularly the relationships among maker, image, and user.

First, current methods for analysing visual images in literacy and communication studies, what have widely become known as "toolkits" for visual analysis (see, e.g., Kress & van Leeuwen, 1996, 2001; also Baldry & Thibault, 2006) are based on a history of images produced in Western contexts. Visual analysis in global literacy research needs to account for more diverse audiences, which means a broader and more situated range of meaning potentials than is currently available in visual analysis "toolkits." As Lister and Wells emphasize, "In practice, it is seldom, if ever, possible to separate the cultures of everyday life from practices of representation, visual or otherwise" (2001, p. 61). Related, because both the production and viewing of images may represent sites of "resistance and recalcitrance" (Rose, 2001, p. 134), a critical approach to analysis is required, one that takes seriously the agency of the image, the social practices, activities, and effects around viewing, and the specific nature of viewing by various audiences, including the researcher as a very unique kind of audience (Rose, 2001). In an attempt to resolve these ongoing issues in my literacy research in Uganda, I blend multimodal ethnography with visual anthropology (see, e.g., Banks & Morphy, 1997) and cultural geography (see Rose, 1996, 2001).

Visual anthropologists contend that film, photography, and drawing can significantly enhance what can be learned about a culture or context (Morphy & Banks, 1997). Their position does not require that visual methods be used in all contexts but, rather, used where appropriate with the caveat that appropriateness may not be obvious from the outset of the study. What visual anthropology adds to a multimodal ethnographic perspective is enhanced opportunities for collaborative and creative data collection and analysis. Traditionally, in visual anthropology researchers rather than research participants have used visual modes for recording culture. Although not initially part of the research design, I began to view my research "participants" as collaborators and put visual tools such as drawing implements and digital cameras in their hands with the invitation to participate in documenting their everyday lives in general but their literacy practices in particular. The participants also provided oral or written accounts of their images, which were integral in our interpretation. The words and images in tandem opened new understandings of the participants' lives and literacy practices, which I discuss in more detail within the vignettes.

In the past few decades, there has also been an increasing interest among cultural geographers in the role of the visual in knowledge construction (e.g., in photographs, maps, diagrams, graphs, and tables) (Rose, 1996). They have much to offer literacy researchers who take a multimodal ethnographic approach, particularly in understanding the maker–image–user relationship. I have found Rose's (1996, 2001) conceptualization of meaning production in cultural geography especially helpful in literacy research. She takes a critical approach, emphasizing that geographers never take visual representations "as straightforward mirrors of reality"; rather, "the meanings of an image are understood as constructed through a range of complex and thoroughly social processes and sites of signification" (1996, p. 4). As she points out, the focus on the complexity of "social processes and sites of signification" is both material and cultural, "forming a network of producers, transmitters, technologies, audiences, exhibitors, media, curators, sites, consumers and critics—to name just some of the actants in this network—all of which make sense of any particular image through complicated, multiple and possibly contradictory codes of signification" (1996, p. 4).

Rose moves from this broad conceptualization of meaning production toward an interpretation of particular images by focusing on what several geographers (e.g., Aitken, 1994; Burgess, 1990) argue are the most important actants within this network: producers, texts, and audiences. Producers are the people and equipment involved in making the image; text refers to the image itself; and audience constitutes all those who look at the image. Visual analysis requires understanding how meaning is produced at each of these three sites and in relation to three interconnected registers: the social, the aesthetic, and the technological (Rose, 2001). The social is the organization of social institutions, social difference, and social subjectivities; the aesthetic refers to visual codes and conventions; and the technological is the equipment involved in the image. Of critical importance here is the need to acknowledge the researcher as one kind of audience for the text they are interpreting. Rose carefully considers the intersections and relationships across three modalities (technological, compositional, and social) and three sites of meaning-making (production, image, and audiencing or viewing) in relation to the uses and meanings of images. The three sites of meaning-making progress from understanding the particular circumstances under which an image is produced (Site 1), to focusing on the image itself as a bounded unit (Site 2), to thinking about how an image is looked at by various audiences in relation to the ways of seeing and the kinds of knowledge they bring to the viewing (Site 3).

Many of the theoretical disagreements about visual analysis across disciplines relate to disputes over which sites of meaning-making are most important and why. I have found it most productive in literacy research to understand meaning-making across production, image, and audience as inextricably linked and recursively relational to each other. In the next section, I describe three vignettes that bring together visual anthropology and Rose's visual methodology with multimodal ethnographic research in three Ugandan communities. Taken together, the visual examples demonstrate the potential of visual methodologies for accessing the emic in literacy studies in a range of contexts.

CURRENT CONTRIBUTIONS AND RESEARCH

The context of this research is Uganda, a landlocked country in East Africa sharing borders with Kenya to the west, Democratic Republic of the Congo to the east, Sudan to the north, and Rwanda and Tanzania to the south. Its population is almost 28 million (United Nations Development Programme Uganda, 2007). The nation is governed by President Museveni, who came to power in 1986 after decades of civil war and unrest. Although there has been violent conflict in northern Uganda since Museveni's presidency began, the rest of the country has been at peace, and significant progress has been made in many areas such as education, economic growth, accountable government and civil service reform, and commitments to poverty reduction and gender equality (Pitamber & Chatterjee, 2005). Despite its gains, however, Uganda is one of the world's most under-resourced countries (United Nations Development Programme Uganda, 2007). Thirty-eight percent of the population lives below the poverty line, and the gross domestic product (GDP) per capita is $320 US.

My work in Uganda began in 2003 with an invitation from a rural, grassroots literacy organization to document the progress of the adult learners in their programme. Since 2003, I have continued to work with various organizations and individuals on a range of longitudinal, qualitative multisite studies, all broadly focused on the literacy ecology of communities. The objective of this body of research was to address the complex relationship between literacy and development. The work was consciously and explicitly collaborative and reciprocal (Lassiter, 2005), contributing in various ways to local capacity building, procurement of resources, and problem solving in both formal and informal education sectors. My theoretical and methodological foundations in NLS, ethnography, multimodality, and visual analysis were integrated with the educational, research, and contextual expertise of East African colleagues. Collaboration began with identifying research questions and continued through research design, data collection, analysis, and publication. The reliability and validity of the research was dependent entirely on these integrated and collaborative relationships (Brock-Utne, 1996).

In bringing together an NLS perspective with multimodal and visual ethnography, I view the visual as social and cultural artifacts and as the "frozen remains of collective action" (Becker, 2007, p. 15). Siegel and Panofsky (2009) stress that interpreting visual texts as artifacts of a particular place and space requires drawing on a range of theoretical frameworks, in other words, a hybrid approach—"a blend or 'mash-up' of theories" (p. 99; see also van Leeuwen, 2011). In each of the vignettes in this section, I use Rose's core methodology as a constructive space for the integration of other visual methodologies to allow for the creation of hybrid or mixed methods of analysis. These hybrid methods allowed me to "explore more fully the range of meanings invested in an image at its different sites" (Rose, 2001, p. 202). Further details of the specific visual methodologies used are discussed in relation to each vignette: (1) images of literacy; (2) HIV/AIDS cartoon messages; and (3) ecomaps as networks of support. Pseudonyms are used throughout.

VIGNETTE 1: DRAWINGS AS WINDOWS ON GIRLS' PERCEPTIONS OF LITERACY

This first vignette details how the use of literacy drawings has the potential to reveal how primary school girls in Uganda understand their community's literacy practices in relation to their own lives and experiences. The study was conducted in Kyato Primary School in Masaka District in the southern part of Uganda (for further details of the study, see Kendrick & Jones, 2008). Participants included 29 girls in Primary 6 (Grade 6). The girls lived a rural lifestyle and, prior to the start of the school day, were responsible for a number of chores related to food production (digging, planting, and harvesting) and home care (fetching water and firewood, preparing food, maintaining their homes and compounds, washing clothes, and caring for siblings). Malaria and other illnesses were common in this area. During leisure time at school, they also learned dancing and singing and enjoyed skipping, talking, and reading together in clusters around the schoolyard.

The use of drawing as a visual method is premised on research that consistently demonstrates children are able to communicate powerful and imaginative ideas and problems through a variety of semiotic systems (Kendrick et al., 2009; Kendrick & McKay, 2002, 2004; Kress, 1997; Weber & Mitchell,

1995; Wetton & McWhirter, 1998). The girls met with a researcher and community-based research assistant to discuss and draw pencil crayon pictures of their ideas and experiences of literacy across the broad contexts of their lives (e.g., in and out of school and in the future). Who or what should be included in the drawings or where they might take place was not specified; rather, the girls were asked to draw pictures of reading and/or writing based on their own ideas and experiences (see Ch. 3, this volume, for methodological details). Because our goal was to solicit the students' own images and ideas, we simply used lead-off questions to open up a topic domain (e.g., what kinds of reading or writing do you do in school or outside of school? How do you think you will use reading or writing in the future?) (see Carspecken, 1996).

In this study, Rose's three sites of meaning-making were integrated with an adaptation of Dyer's (1982) checklist for interpreting what the drawings as signs might mean within this particular sociocultural context. With the assistance of Harriet Mutonyi (at the time of the study, a Ugandan PhD student), the images were coded according to the following categories: representations of bodies (age, male or female, race, hair, body, size, and looks), representations of manner (expression, eye contact, and pose), representations of activity (touch, body movement, and positional communication), and representations of props and setting. Working back and forth across sites of meaning-making, we concentrated first on creating a description of the visual image as a bounded unit (site of the image); this included written or oral information that the students provided about their images. We then worked to establish narrative threads that wove together observational and interview data collected as part of the site of production and in relation to our own positioning as viewers of the image (site of audiencing). Critical to this process was a negotiated interpretation of the images, filtered through our own preconceived understandings and subjectivities as researchers. I present two examples (Hannah's and Nassozi's drawings) that are representative of the predominant literacy practices featured in the collection as a whole.

Hannah's Image of Literacy

Hannah's drawing is a self-portrait (see Figure 4.1). Although she is not in her school uniform, she is dressed formally in a dress and shoes that would be typical of secondary school girls in this area who travel home from boarding school on weekends or during holidays. Her depiction of herself in "high fashion" clothing, particularly the shoes, may also be reflective of a desired future lifestyle that affords her material goods that she does not currently possess.

The image of the bench under the tree is a common one in rural areas, particularly on school grounds. It is a typical reading or study environment; students sit under trees, sheltered from the sun, to read school or leisure materials or to prepare for examinations at the end of term. Hannah's solitary positioning here may be indicative of her need to claim a private space away

Figure 4.1 Hannah

from other distractions. Studying in private signals that schoolwork is taken seriously, which is reinforced by Hannah's concentrated facial expression and upright posture. She clearly labels her reading material *Young Talk*, which is a monthly national newspaper for youth that communicates information about HIV/AIDS and other sexual health issues. *Young Talk*, a common reading resource in Hannah's school, requires a high level of English language ability, which may reflect her desire to become part of the English literacy community because of the increased life opportunities it will afford her. As she explained in writing, she is reading *Young Talk* "to know about the [English] words."[2]

We see the narrative Hannah composed in the drawing as representative of her imagined "freedoms" (Sen, 1999) in relation to economics, education, and status in her society. She portrays herself as a well-dressed, young woman who is literate in English. English is the medium of instruction from Primary 4 (Year 4) onwards. Students have many challenges learning English: They have limited opportunities to use and maintain the language and infrequent access to English reading materials. From a global perspective, literacy in Uganda is strongly linked to the hegemony of English, and there is status associated with using the language. Hannah also portrays herself as someone knowledgeable about issues such as HIV/AIDS and early sexual activity; there is power associated with this knowledge because these are two possible barriers to Hannah in attaining an education and a comfortable lifestyle. What this example illustrates is the potential of the visual to make visible both real and imagined "literate" identities in ways that language alone cannot.

Gertrude's Image of Literacy

Gertrude's drawing includes two images of self: standing on the left and sitting in a chair on the right (see Figure 4.2). In both, she is holding a book. The images read as a moving sequence that shows Gertrude coming to sit under the tree. In the first frame, she is walking toward the chair, carrying a book; in the second, she is sitting and reading. She explained that she is reading an English book "to study the word." Similar to Hannah,

Figure 4.2 Gertrude

Gertrude's drawing emphasizes the importance of English to education in this cultural context. The inclusion of the word *education* and images of books on the trunk and at the base of the tree may also profile the tree as a signifier of knowledge acquired through formal education in general and book reading in English in particular.

As noted in Hannah's drawing, occupying the space under a tree represents a claim to a private space, ownership of one's own place to read. Gertrude, however, is clearly occupying a chair. In this rural community, sitting in a chair is often the privilege of men. Her occupation of the chair as a young girl is a claim to status and power in her community, an imagined action rather than something she may actually do. Her formal style of dress and high-heeled shoes indicate that she is most likely away from home. The image is one of a well-educated woman who has the economic resources for material goods such as fashionable clothing and books and whose status allows her to occupy important positions (e.g., the chair); we see these as the imagined "freedoms" (Sen, 1999) and imagined identities (Norton, 2013) she aspires to in the future in relation to her investment in learning English.

Both Hannah and Gertrude position themselves as readers in the world. In this rural area, few adults read and write in English, and both a reader identity and the language of English carry considerable status. The inclusion of props such as *Young Talk*, English books, and science texts are also symbolic of the status associated with membership in the English literate world. The vast majority of the drawings in this collection depicted settings other than school, and particularly outdoor settings, which is reflective of the multiple contexts in which reading and writing take place in this community. Students also included participants other than themselves, most typically friends and siblings. Strikingly absent from all of the drawings were teachers, parents, and other adults as mediators of literacy, which may suggest that for these students, peers and siblings play particularly important roles in scaffolding English literacy learning. Gregory (2001) describes this interaction as a synergy, a "unique reciprocity whereby siblings [and peers] act as adjuvants in each other's learning" (p. 309). The students portrayed themselves as actively engaged in the reading process. It is noteworthy that writing as a literacy practice was virtually non-existent other than exam writing. In Uganda, where social interaction historically has been the predominant means of communication, writing, which often is considered a very private and individualistic activity, may not be viewed as an integral part of everyday social activities.

VIGNETTE 2: HEALTH LITERACY AND HIV/AIDS KNOWLEDGE

This second example is taken from a study focused on the health literacy knowledge of Senior 3 (Grade 11) biology students, specifically in relation to HIV/AIDS (writing and analysis were part of a mentorship grant with Harriet Mutonyi; see Mutonyi & Kendrick, 2010, 2011, for further study details).

Senior 3 classes were selected because this age group is considered high risk for contracting HIV/AIDS (Uganda AIDS Commission, 2007), and the topic is also part of the Senior 3 biology curriculum. As part of a questionnaire on HIV/AIDS, students were asked to take on the role of public educators and propose a new public service message about HIV/AIDS. The specific question was: "What would be your own slogan for HIV/AIDS? Illustrate in a cartoon form the message your slogan would convey about HIV/AIDS. Explain the message your cartoon is conveying." Cartoons rather than drawings were selected because the students indicated they associated the word *drawing* with "artistic" drawing, and they were not "talented" in that way. In contrast, cartooning (what they called "stick images") allowed them to draw without attending to aesthetic positioning and spatial relationships. For these students, cartooning was a familiar mode of communication used extensively in public education campaigns that target youth. As such, the students did not have preconceived notions of school-sanctioned standards for how cartoons should look or function.

The analysis in this vignette brings together Rose's methodology with Warburton's (1998) analytic framework for interpreting cartoons as mediated public messages. Warburton uses four stages of analysis beginning with an initial description of the image itself, followed by immediate connotation, systemic connotation, and establishment of narrative threads. Our collaborative interpretation of the images traverses Rose's (2001) sites of production, image, and audience in relation to Warburton's four stages of description. The students' own voices, evident in their written text (i.e., the inclusion of cartoon titles or captions), were critical to our interpretive process. Our initial description focused on identifying the visual and textual material contained in the cartoon and who and what are represented (site of image). Immediate connotation addressed what the cartoon might mean to the general public and what the image might signify publically (site of audiencing). Systemic connotation moved toward identifying the place and status of the cartoon with respect to the communication system or systems it is part of (site of production in terms of the wider society). Finally, we sought to establish narrative threads by synthesizing across sites of meaning-making to identify what or who the cartoon was intended for and the relationship between the cartoon and broader discourses on HIV/AIDS. We also draw somewhat on Kress and van Leeuwen's (1996) participant representation and interaction framework. Meanings at each stage were negotiated and co-constructed by both researchers. We present two images, Janice's and Tolophina's, as illustrative examples.

Janice's Cartoon

Janice's cartoon depicts the relationship between sexual violence and HIV/AIDS in graphic simplicity (see Figure 4.3). What immediately captures the viewer's attention is her explicit depiction of a young girl fleeing from a man who is attempting to rape her. She includes a plus sign (+) beside the man's

Figure 4.3 Janice

body, indicating that he is HIV positive, and the disturbing statement: "I want to rape you fast come here," to which the girl responds: "What! Uh . . . Oh, my Lord Jesus." Rape of young people has been reported as one of the major vulnerabilities to HIV/AIDS infection (MoH, 2006). The image draws attention to a commonly held belief in Uganda that having sex with a virgin will cure HIV/AIDS. Such myths have led to many infected persons raping young people under their care in the hope of an immediate cure (MoES/PIASCY, 2005). Janice captures the brutality of this practice in visual form. Open discussion of rape in Uganda is very uncommon, and many occurrences go unreported. This cartoon highlights the issue through the power of the visual, a more socially and culturally acceptable mode than language for communicating difficult knowledge. The example points to the need to consider carefully alternative and preferred modes of communication for research study participants and co-investigators in literacy studies and to challenge assumptions about the privileging of language in data collection methods.

Tolophina's Cartoon

Tolophina's cartoon is a narrative involving three characters: her friend Susan, an unnamed man, and Susan's boyfriend, George. She frames the narrative in terms of her own relationship with Susan: "I am worried my friend Susan [has] HIV/AIDS" and "Susan on streets with other men b'se [because] she had arrived at Kampala." On the left side of the cartoon, we see Susan and a man engaged in a sexual transaction (see Figure 4.4), with Susan asking, "How much are you going to pay me?" Her extended arm as a gesture directed toward the man simultaneously communicates the initiation of sexual solicitation. The man, who is facing away from Susan, is given a more passive role in the interaction. In the second frame of the cartoon, Susan's body positioning creates a direct line to George, her boyfriend, and again establishes her active role in the interaction. George's body directed away from Susan adds to the narrative the possibility of someone or something that is not represented in the picture. In the final frame of the narrative, Susan is represented above George in a potential position of power over him. The representation of Susan in an active role in initiating transactional

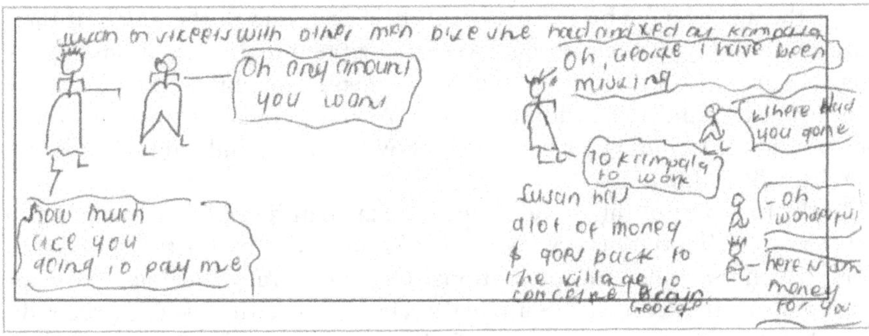

Figure 4.4 Tolophina

relationships to earn money and maintaining romantic relationships with the lure of money emphasizes the vulnerability of all those who have sex with sex trade workers rather than the vulnerability of the sex trade workers themselves. This notion of vulnerability is emphasized further by the unknown in relation to George's gaze and body positioning, which points out-of-frame in both the second and third sequence of the narrative.

The narrative portrayed in Tolophina's cartoon also shows the link between socioeconomic status and the spread of HIV/AIDS and how poverty is a contributor across urban and rural sexual networks. The network begins with George and Susan as friends in their rural village and then expands when Susan goes to Kampala to work as a sex trade workers. Girls from poor families sometimes resort to working in the sex trade to survive, and in Uganda, this practice is most predominant in Kampala. Because of these circumstances, Tolophina is concerned that Susan has been exposed to HIV infection. George, on the other hand, is portrayed as innocent and in love with Susan, who takes advantage of his trust. He happily accepts the money she earns as a sex trade worker, possibly because he is also poor. Despite central messages of sexual faithfulness in the Ugandan HIV/AIDS campaign, this cartoon portrays some of the circumstances under which partners are unfaithful. Tolophina depicts the girl as an initiating actor rather than a victim. She also portrays the rural male as vulnerable to the city-savvy female. In this context, girls and women are more likely to be blamed for enticing sexual interaction or violence rather than directing any responsibility toward men as part of the sexual transaction or more broadly pointing to issues of poverty as a factor.

VIGNETTE 3: NETWORKS OF SUPPORT IN CHILD-HEADED FAMILIES

In a third study (conducted in collaboration with Doris Kakuru, a Ugandan sociologist), I focus on the funds of knowledge of children living in child-headed families in the Rakai District. Child-headed families are children under the age of 17 who are living on their own due to the death of their parents, inability of their parents to care for them (e.g., due to physical or mental illness, additions, etc.), or abandonment. The objective in this study was to understand the children's ability to navigate survival both in and out of school, including learning new knowledge (for full study details, see Kendrick & Kakuru, 2012).

In the first part of this vignette, we use Hartman's (1995) ecomapping to make visible children's everyday funds of knowledge and networks of support, which we argue are foundational to their literacy learning. Ecomaps are diagrams that consist of an inner circle or centre (in this case, the individual child), surrounded by other circles representing the elements in their social network. Lines connecting the inner circle and each individual circle depict the strength of the relationship between the individuals and the flow of resources (e.g., a thick line or multiple lines depicts a strong relationship, whereas a thin or broken line depicts a less-prominent relationship). The word *ecomap* is derived from the word *ecology*, and the tool developed by Hartman uses the human elements of ecology to represent the social relationships and social systems that people create to enable effective interactions with the physical and social environment in which they live and work.

Ecomapping Networks of Support

Ecomaps have been used in a wide variety of family research, from clinical to ethnographic studies (see, e.g., Ray & Street, 2005; Rempel, Neufeld, & Kushner, 2007), although their predominant application has been in family therapy and clinical family nursing studies. The ecomaps as a visual reveal critical information about the social networks of an individual or family and the nature of the bonds within these networks (see, e.g., Hartman, 1995); in our case, it makes visible the children's knowledge sources and potential literacy supporters.

The illustrative example included here features one family of five children: Ibra (age 12), Winnie (age 10), Manny (age 6), Paul (age 4), and David (age 3). Their father died in 2004, followed by their mother two years later. Because the parents died at home, without any medical care, their cause of death was not documented. Prior to the parents' deaths, the family had relocated from another district to the Rakai District. We speculate that the relocation was most likely a result of the stigma of living with HIV/AIDS in their home community and that further stigma associated with the death of their parents made it impossible for the children to return to the area where their extended family lived. The children were therefore quite isolated both from extended family and within their new community. To better understand their systems of social support and means of learning new knowledge, we provided markers and paper and asked the two older children, Winnie and Ibra, to construct an ecomap. The purpose of the activity was to reveal hidden networks of support that may not have been evident in

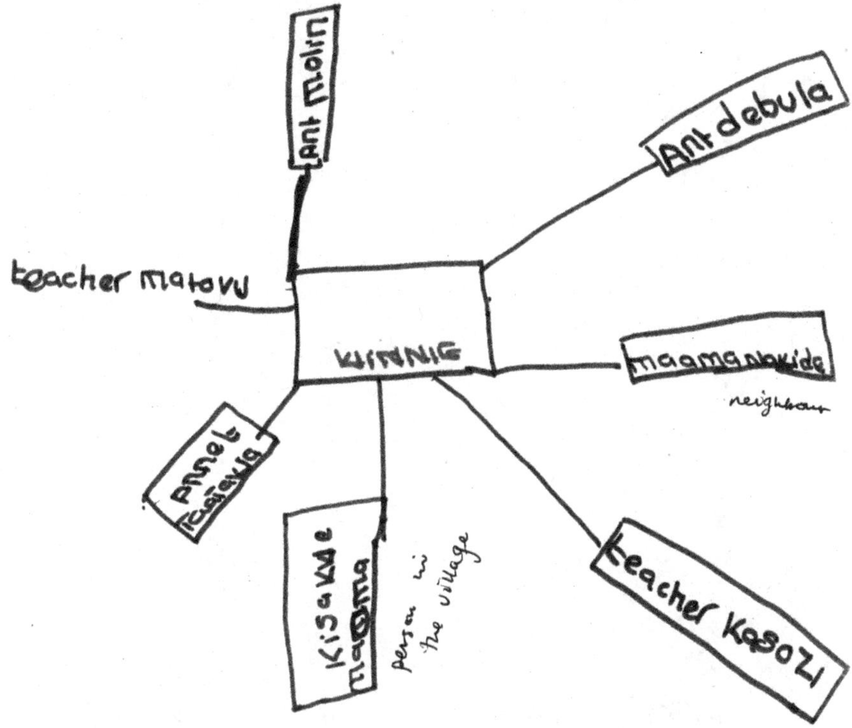

Figure 4.5 Winnie

our interviews and observations. At the centre of the map, Winnie and Ibra wrote their names then drew lines connected to rectangular boxes. In each rectangular box, they were asked to write the names of people who support them in any way.

Winnie created two maps. The first identified four individuals, one whose name she struggled to recall. She asked for a second paper to make a new map, which was similar to her first but with the addition of both my research assistant's name ("Ant Debbie") and mine ("Ant Morin [Maureen]") (see Figure 4.5). Winnie also identified two teachers (but only one name is in a box), the father of her friend Annet (whose name she could not recall on her first map), and their nearest neighbour. Ibra's ecomap (see Figure 4.6) includes the same neighbour his sister identified, the same two "aunts" (Debbie and Maureen), as well as the name of a person he knew in the village.

If we focus on these ecomaps as visual products alone (site of the image), there appears to be a small network of supporters for the children. Yet, if we simultaneously consider the site of production in relation to the image, a more nuanced story emerges. What is most telling is that production took considerable time because neither Ibra nor Winnie could think of any people

Figure 4.6 Ibra

or organizations that supported them. The first name listed by Winnie was a neighbour who on limited occasions had cared for David, the youngest member of the family. Following this, she paused for several minutes and finally decided to list the names of two of her teachers. When we followed this up with brief interviews at the school, the teachers had little awareness of the children's home situation. It may be that the school's permission for Winnie and her brothers to attend school without paying fees earned the two teachers a place on her ecomap. The fourth person Winnie listed, the father of her friend Annet, is a man who had on one occasion helped the children repair the leaky roof in their house. My name and Debbie's, the research assistant, were added at the end, after Winnie asked if it was okay to include us. My name is connected with a heavier line, most likely because of advocacy that provided some essential resources. Debbie provided ongoing support with teaching the children a range of skills, including how to grow and prepare food. For almost the full duration of the session (20 minutes), Ibra's ecomap (see Figure 4.6) remained largely blank with the exception of his own name and the neighbour's. Also telling was that Winnie took the lead in this activity, even though she was younger.

"What Makes You Happy?"

The second part of this vignette focuses on two of the other children in this family, Manny (6) and Paul (4). An important aspect of our data collection was to create an opportunity for the children to share positive aspects of their lives, given their difficult circumstances and the nature of the larger study. We asked them to use drawing to respond to the question "What makes you happy?" From a literacy perspective, this activity not only provided a window on what mattered to these children, including their hope for the future, but in this case, it also made visible the unique knowledge exchange between these two young brothers. At the time of the study, Paul had just started primary school. Manny, who was hearing impaired, had not had opportunities to develop his oral language abilities and was struggling significantly in his regular classroom placement. During the drawing activity, although the boys sat on opposite sides of their front room, their drawings are strikingly similar (see Figures 4.7 and 4.8). Both drawings capture

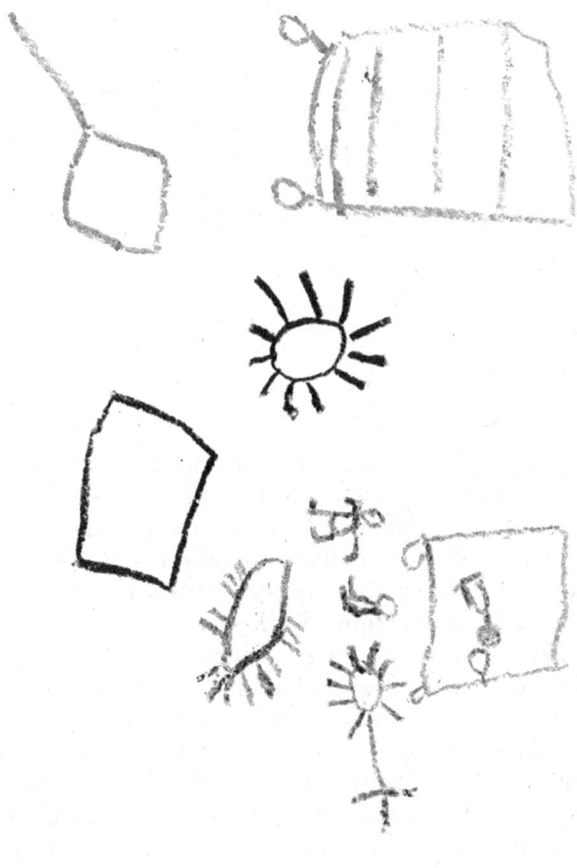

Figure 4.7 Paul

Figure 4.8 Manny

what is happening in the immediate moment. They include a bed, chair, children, a baby, a sleeping mat, and a sun—signs that represent family. The drawings alerted us to the remarkable connection that these brothers shared, and we also began to observe in other situations the degree to which Manny relied almost exclusively on his younger brother Paul to help him understand and successfully navigate his immediate social environment. We were able to share this critical information with the headmaster at the children's local school, which had no provision for hearing impaired children. The headmaster placed both boys in the same classroom, and our follow-up months later indicated that both boys were meeting with success at school.

What becomes visible in looking across the site of production, the images, and the site of viewing is the backstory, the story behind the scenes that provides a more nuanced understanding of the children's networks of support and foundations for literacy in their daily lives. By working across sites of meaning-making, we were able to raise questions about both the challenges these children face and the nature of the strategies they employ in navigating both school and community expectations, which provided critical information in advocating for this young family and their educational needs.

RECOMMENDATIONS FOR RESEARCH PRACTICE

The field of literacy studies has changed significantly in the past decade. It has taken a semiotic turn, which requires that researchers rethink traditional research methodologies to "bring knowing to the surface of consciousness, to help [participants] transform what they know, remember, sense, hear, feel, and believe into a paragraph of writing, a lively dialogue, a scrapbook of images, an academic essay" (Stein, 2000, p. 66) in new, creative, and multimodal ways. Siegel and Panofsky argue,

> The unsettled status of the field appears to be a productive moment of experimentation, invention, and problem-posing as researchers design analytic approaches that draw on a range of theoretical frameworks relevant to their research interests, purposes, and questions. . . . Analyzing multimodality requires a hybrid approach—a blend or "mash-up" of theories.
>
> (2009, p. 99)

Inherent in the design of analytic approaches to my collaborative literacy research is a complex interplay among research and pedagogical questions, theoretical frameworks, and methods of interpreting visual images, integral to which is meaningful collaboration with co-investigators and participants who contribute to understanding the relationship between the maker or producer and user or viewer of visual images in a given society.

In the research reported in the three vignettes in this chapter, negotiated emic and etic meanings between researchers and co-investigators, collaborators, or participants help make visible "the plural, messy, contested, and even creative nature of our discourse with the visual and with images, and the manner in which this is a site of struggle over what something means" (Lister & Wells, 2001, p. 73). Each visual example offers a "sideways glance at literacy" (Kendrick, 2005) that reveals new understandings. Vignette 1 illustrates how the visual has the potential to complement other modes of data collection in literacy studies. In both Hannah's and Gertrude's images of literacy we simultaneously glimpse the here and now of their social world in relation to their imaginings of the future. Vignette 2 demonstrates the importance of the visual in studies that tap into culturally and socially difficult knowledge. In the context in our example, difficult knowledge associated with HIV/AIDS (e.g., violence, disease, stigma, and sexual practices) is communicated more easily through drawings than through talk. The cartoon images about HIV/AIDS are unique cultural artifacts that both synthesize and amplify cultural and personal knowledge (Warburton & Saunders, 1996). They allow for the expression of a much fuller range of human emotion and experience than spoken or written communication alone (Kress & van Leeuwen, 1996) and simultaneously integrate and transcend taboo ways of discussing sexuality. Vignette 3 emphasizes the critical need to not privilege any one of the three sites of meaning-making in the interpretation of an image. If, as Collier argues, images "give birth to stories" (2001, p. 46), then we need to discover the whole story by tracing it from producer to audience.

I argue that the interpretation of visual images as data in literacy research requires a collaborative and hybrid approach to more fully consider the unique sociocultural context of a study and to uncover nuances of practices that were not visible through linguistic modes alone. The analyses help raise questions about the possible meanings of an image in relation to broader theories and discourses on literacy and identity. The visual examples also provide evidence that in all cultural contexts the visual, like literacy, is a situated communicative practice.

"THICK DESCRIPTION" IN LITERACY STUDIES: WHAT THE VISUAL CAN OFFER

New Literacy Studies (NLS) frame not only the studies featured in this chapter, but mark a rich new tradition in the study of the nature of literacy. NLS focus on literacy as a social practice, which necessitates "the recognition of multiple literacies [and multiple modes as I argue throughout this book], varying according to time and space, but also contested in relations of power. NLS, then, takes nothing for granted with respect to literacy and the social practices with which it becomes associated, problematizing what counts as literacy at any time and place" (Street, 2003, p. 77). From this tradition, the question of what counts as literacy is most typically addressed ethnographically, underscoring the description of literacy practices of everyday life and challenging autonomous approaches emphasizing decontextualized skills. According to Stein (2007), "a key contribution of New Literacy Studies has been to provide evidence of how literacy varies across cultural time and space" by describing "different occasions, contexts and concepts which constitute people's relations to and engagements with literacy, research in the NLS, often ethnographic in style, provides 'thick descriptions' (Geertz, 1983) of the complex, changing uses of multiple literacies embedded in particular domains or settings" (p. 30).

"Thick description" distinguishes between a "thin description" of, for example, a symbolic action, and a "thick description," which includes the context. Geertz gives the example of discerning the difference between a wink (thick description) and a twitch (thin description), which requires more than simply relating what happened. Such a distinction requires judgments, assumptions, and explanations about *why* someone behaved as they did, *what* they were trying to communicate, and *for whom* (Knowles, 2011). Thick description requires interpretation that microscopically traces the manner in which meaning is ascribed. As Lincoln and Guba (1985) take up the idea, thick description is a way of achieving an external validity through the description of a phenomenon in sufficient enough detail that readers can evaluate the ethnographer's conclusions and potentially compare them to other times, settings, situations, and people.

If the goal of ethnographic research is to provide a thick description that explicates how humans are suspended in "webs of significance" (p. 5), webs that get knotted into one another as part of a shared "imaginative universe" in which people's actions represent signs (p. 13), then as literacy researchers, we need to ask how we can best operationalize multimodal "webs of significance." Relatedly, if we are to take seriously Street's (2003) point that NLS "takes nothing for granted," then we need to address the ways in which participants in literacy studies think and express meaning multimodally and the ways in which they remember and store events and experiences using modes other than language. A starting point is to consider what the visual can offer literacy studies. In each of the vignettes included in this chapter, the visual enables participants to tell their stories differently and to tell their stories in modes beyond language. Many of their stories include "difficult knowledge" (e.g., issues related to sexual violence, sexual solicitation, and family loss and bereavement) or knowledge and experience that would be taboo to express in language. Here, the visual serves a "microscopic" function by making visible what participants would not have been able to express in interviews or that would not have been accessible to me through observation. From an ethnographic perspective, the images also provide both a sense of place and a sense of the human condition, capturing the affective in a way that is unique to the visual. From the perspective of thick description, "images may have an ineffable kinesthetic, sensory, or affective force that communicates what words can't" (Tucker, 2014, n.p.), making it easier for participants and researchers to reach a wider audience and a much more textured understanding of literacy across time and space in the 21st century. If literacy researchers are to understand fully the multimodal nature of literacy in current times (see, e.g., Kress, 2010; van Leeuwen, 2011), they must engage in multimodal data collection that invites their participants to communicate their lives and experiences in modes beyond language. As van Leeuwen (2011) argues,

> Spoken language cannot be adequately understood without taking non-verbal communication into account; and that many forms of contemporary written language cannot be adequately understood unless we look, not just at language, but also at images, layout, typography and colour. In the past twenty or so years this led to the development of multimodality as a field of study investigating the common as well as the distinct

> properties of the different modes in the multimodal mix and the way they integrate in multimodal texts and communicative events.
>
> (p. 668)

FUTURE DIRECTIONS

Thirty years ago, Harste, Woodword, and Burke urged literacy researchers to abandon "a 'verbocentric' (Eco, 1976) view of literacy and to adopt a semiotic one, in which the orchestration of all signifying structures from all available communication systems in the event have a part" (1984, p. 208). New relationships among word, image, and sound in 21st century literacy practices mean that literacy studies are now dependent on understanding relationships among and across communicative modes. Literacy studies have become *multimodal studies*, and written language can no longer be privileged. A key requirement for researchers engaged in multimodal studies is to experiment with modes as part of data collection and to consider carefully across culture, place, and space the situated ways in which what can be expressed in language might be more aptly expressed through the visual, the auditory, or the kinesthetic. In other words, a culture's range of semiotic modes needs to be both theoretically *and* methodologically considered from a social practices perspective. This consideration involves understanding more fully how modalities such as the visual take different forms and functions depending on the user and context. If the goal of literacy as social practice research is to reveal rather than disguise the cultural and ideological assumptions that underpin modes of communication across cultures, then theory and method need to be more closely aligned. The use of visual methodologies in literacy and multimodal studies provides one such example.

NOTE

1. This chapter is an extended version of Kendrick, M. (2015). The affordances and challenges of visual methodologies in literacy studies. In J. Rowsell & K. Pahl, *The Routledge Handbook of Literacy Studies* (pp. 619–633). New York, NY: Routledge.
2. *Young Talk* is a newspaper produced by a Ugandan NGO. Its focus is on educating youth about sexuality, reproductive health, and preventing HIV.

REFERENCES

Aitken, S. C. (1994). I'd rather watch the movie than read the book. *Journal of Geography in Higher Education, 18*(3), 291–307.

Baldry, A., & Thibault, P. (2006). *Multimodal analysis and text transcription*. London, UK: Equinox.

Banks, M., & Morphy, H. (Eds.) (1997). *Rethinking visual anthropology*. New Haven, CT: Yale University Press.

Barton, D., & Hamilton, M. (1998). *Local literacies: Reading and writing in one community*. New York, NY: Routledge.

Baynham, M. (1995). *Literacy practices: Investigating literacy in social contexts*. London, UK: Longman.

Becker, H.S. (2007). *Telling about society*. Chicago: University of Chicago Press.

Brock-Utne, B. (1996). Reliability and validity in qualitative research within education in Africa. *International Review of Education, 42*(6), 605–621.

Burgess, J. (1990). The production and consumption of environmental meanings in the mass media: A research agenda for the 1990s. *Transactions of the Institute of British Geographers, 15*(2), 139–161.

Carrington, V. (2003). "I'm in a bad mood. Let's go shopping": Interactive dolls, consumer culture and a "glocalized" model of literacy. *Journal of Early Childhood Literacy, 3*(1), 83–98.

Carspecken, P. F. (1996). *Critical ethnography in educational research*. London, UK: Routledge.

Collier, M. (2001). Approaches to analysis in visual anthropology. In T. van Leeuwen & C. Jewitt (Eds.), *Handbook of visual analysis* (pp. 35–60). London: Sage.

de la Piedra, M.T. (2006). Literacies and Quecha oral language: Connecting sociocultural worlds and linguistic resources for biliteracy development. *Journal of Early Childhood Literacy*, 6(3), 383–406.

Dicks, B., Flewitt, R., Lancaster, L., & Pahl, K. (2011). Multimodality and ethnography: Working at the intersection. *Qualitative Research, 11*(3), 227–237.

Dyer, G. (1982). *Advertising as communication*. London, UK: Routledge.

Fairclough, N. (Ed.). (1992). *Critical language awareness*. London, UK: Longman.

Gregory, E. (1998). Siblings as mediators of literacy in linguistic minority communities. *Language and Education: An International Journal, 12* (1), 33–55.

Gregory, E. (2001). Sisters and Brothers as Language and Literacy Teachers: Synergy Between Siblings. *Journal of Early Childhood Literacy, 1*, 301–322.

Hamilton, M. (2000). Expanding the new literacy studies: Using photographs to explore literacy as social practice. In D. Barton, M. Hamiliton, & R. Ivanič (Eds.), *Situated literacies: Reading and writing in context* (pp. 16–34). London, UK: Routledge.

Harste, J. C., Woodward, V., & Burke, C. (1984). *Language stories and literacy lessons*. Portsmouth, NH: Heinemann.

Hartman, A. (1995). Diagrammatic assessment of family relationships. *Families in Society: The Journal of Contemporary Human Services, 76*(2), 111–122.

Heath, S. B. (1983). *Ways with words: Language, life, and work in communities and classroom*. Cambridge, UK: Cambridge University Press.

Heath, S. B., & Wollach, R. (2007). Vision for learning: History, theory, and affirmation. In J. Flood, S. B. Heath, & D. Lapp (Eds.), *Handbook of research on teaching literacy through the communicative and visual arts* (Vol. II, pp. 3–12). New York, NY: Lawrence Erlbaum.

Hodge, R., & Jones, K. (1996). Photographs in collaborative research: "Insider" "outsider" images and understandings of multilingual literacy practices. Centre for the Study of Language in Social Life Working Paper 83, Lancaster University.

Hull, G., & Katz, M. L. (2006). Crafting an agentive self: Case studies of digital storytelling. *Research in the Teaching of English, 14*(1), 43–81.

Kendrick, M. (2005). Playing house: A sideways glance at literacy and identity in early childhood. *Journal of Early Childhood Literacy, 5*(1), 5–28.

Kendrick, M., Early, M., & Chemjor, W. (2013). Integrated literacies in a rural Kenyan girls' secondary school journalism club. *Research in the Teaching of English, 47*(4), 391–419.

Kendrick, M., & Jones, S. (2008). Girls' visual representations of literacy in a rural Ugandan community. *Canadian Journal of Education, 31*(2), 371–402.

Kendrick, M., Jones, S., Mutonyi, H., & Norton, B. (2009). Using drawing, photography, and drama to enhance students' English language learning in Uganda. In M. Dantas-Whitney & S. Rilling (Eds.), *Authenticity in the language classroom and beyond: Children and adolescent learners* (pp. 181–197). Alexandria, VA: TESOL.

Kendrick, M., & Kakuru, D. (2012). Funds of knowledge in child-headed households: A Ugandan case study. *Childhood: A Journal of Global Child Research, 19*(3), 397–413.

Kendrick, M., & McKay, R. (2002). Uncovering literacy narratives through children's drawings: An illustrative example. *Canadian Journal of Education, 27*(1), 45–60.

Kendrick, M., & McKay, R. (2004). Drawings as an alternative way of understanding young children's constructions of literacy. *Journal of Early Childhood Literacy, 4*(1), 109–128.

Kendrick, M., & Mutonyi, H. (2007). Meeting the challenge of health literacy in rural Uganda: The critical role of women and local modes of communication. *Diaspora, Indigenous, and Minority Education, 1*(4), 265–283.

Knowles, C. (2011). Thick description: History and anthropology. Retrieved from http://howitreallywas.typepad.com/how_it_really_was/2011/06/thick-description-history-and-anthropology.html

Kress, G. (1997). *Before writing: Rethinking the paths to literacy*. London, UK: Routledge.

Kress, G. (2010). *Multimodality: A social semiotic approach to contemporary communication*. London, UK: Routledge.

Kress, G., & Jewitt, C. (2003). Introduction. In C. Jewitt & G. Kress (Eds.), *Multimodal literacy* (pp. 1–18). New York, NY: Peter Lang.

Kress, G., & van Leeuwen, T. (1996). *Reading images: The grammar of visual design*. London, UK: Routledge.

Kress, G., & van Leeuwen, T. (2001). *Multimodal discourse: The modes and media of contemporary communication*. New York: Oxford Press.

Lassiter, L. E. (2005). *The Chicago guide to collaborative ethnography*. Chicago, IL: University of Chicago Press.

Lincoln, Y. S., & Guba, E. G. (1985). *Naturalistic inquiry*. Newbury Park, CA: Sage Publications.

Lister, M., & Wells, L. (2001). Seeing beyond belief: Cultural studies as an approach to analyzing the visual. In T. van Leeuwen & C. Jewitt (Eds.), *Handbook of visual analysis* (pp. 61–91). London, UK: Sage.

Mannion, G., & Ivanic, R. (2007). Mapping literacy practices: Theory, methodology, and methods. *International Journal of Qualitative Studies in Education, 20*(1), 15–30.

Morphy, H., & Banks, M. (1997). Introduction: Rethinking visual anthropology. In M. Banks & H. Morphy (Eds.), *Rethinking visual anthropology* (pp. 1–35). New Haven, CT: Yale University Press.

Ministry of Education and Sports (MoES)/PIASCY. (2005). *Lower post primary: Student handbook on HIV/AIDS*. Kampala: MoES.

Ministry of Health (MoH). (2006). *2004–05 Uganda HIV/AIDS Sero-behavioural survey*. Kampala, Uganda: Ministry of Health.

Moll, L., Amanti, C., Neff, D., & Gonzàlez, N. (2005). Funds of knowledge for teaching: Using a qualitative approach to connect homes and classrooms. In N. Gonzàlez, L. Moll, & C. Amanti (Eds.), *Funds of knowledge: Theorizing practices in households, communities, and classrooms* (pp. 71–89). Mahwah, NJ: Lawrence Erlbaum. (Original work published 1992)

Mutonyi, H., & Kendrick, M. (2010). Ugandan students' visual representations of health literacies: A focus on HIV/AIDS knowledge. In C. Higgins & B. Norton (Eds.), *Language and HIV/AIDS* (pp. 38–62). Clevedon, UK: Multilingual Matters.

Mutonyi, H., & Kendrick, M. (2011). Cartoon drawing as a means of accessing what students know about HIV/AIDS: An alternative method. *Visual Communication Journal, 10*(2), 231–249.

New London Group. (1996). A pedagogy of multiliteracies: Designing social futures. *Harvard Educational Review, 66*(1), 60–92.

Norton, B. (2013). *Identity and language learning: Extending the conversation* (2nd ed.). Bristol, UK: Multilingual Matters.

Pahl, K. (2003). Children's text-making at home: Transforming meaning across modes. Introduction. In C. Jewitt & G. Kress (Eds.), *Multimodal literacy* (pp. 139–154). New York: Peter Lang.

Pitamber, S., & Chatterjee, S. (2005). Uganda: Multi-sector country gender profile. Agriculture and rural development, north east and south region (ONAR). (African Development Fund Publication No. Multi Sector Country #32F8E4. pdf). Retrieved from http://www.afdb.org/pls/portal/url/ITEM/F5BB3A8937FD 0ED9E030A8C0668C1BE0Ray, R. A., & Street, A. F. (2005). Ecomapping: An innovative research tool for nurses. *Journal of Advanced Nursing, 50*(5), 545–552.

Rempel, G.R., Neufeld, A., & Kushner, K.E. (2007). Interactive use of genograms and ecomaps in family caregiving research. *Journal of Family Nursing,* 13(4), 403–419.

Rose, G. (1996). Teaching visualised geographies: Towards a methodology for the interpretation of visual materials. *Journal of Geography in Higher Education, 20*(3), 281–294.

Rose, G. (2001). *Visual methodologies.* London, UK: Sage.

Sen, A. (1999). *Development as freedom.* New York, NY: Anchor Books.

Siegel, M., & Panofsky, C. P. (2009). Designs for multimodality in literacy studies: Explorations in analysis. In K. M. Leander, D. W. Rowe, D. Dickinson, R. Jimenez, M. Hundley, & V. Risko (Eds.), *58th National Reading Conference yearbook* (pp. 99–111). Oak Creek, WI: National Reading Conference.

Smythe, S., & Toohey, K. (2009). Investigating sociohistorical contexts and practices through a community scan: A Canadian Punjabi Sikh example. *Language and Education, 21*(1), 37–57.

Stein, P. (2000). Rethinking resources: Multimodal pedagogies in the ESL classroom. *TESOL Quarterly, 34*(2), 333–336.

Stein, P. (2007). *Multimodal pedagogies in diverse classrooms: Representation, rights, and resources.* London, UK: Routledge.

Street, B. (1984). *Literacy in theory and practice.* Cambridge, UK: Cambridge University Press.

Street, B. (2003). What's "new" in the new literacy studies? Critical approaches to literacy in theory and practice. *Current Issues in Comparative Education, 5*(2), 77–91.

Tucker, A. (2014). Psychocultural cinema: The state of visual anthropology and multi-modal ethnograph. Retrieved from http://psychoculturalcinema.com/the-state-of-visual-anthropology-and-multi-modal-ethnography-a-report-from-the-screening-scholarship-media-festival-2014-part-2-of-2/

Uganda AIDS Commission (UAC) (2007) *National HIV and AIDS Strategic Plan 2007/08 – 2011/12.* Kampala: UAC.

United Nations Development Programme Uganda. (2007). UNDP Uganda. Retrieved from http://www.undp.or.ug/aboutug.php

van Leeuwen, T. (2011). Multimodality. In J. Simpson (Ed.), *The Routledge handbook of applied linguistics* (pp. 668–682). London, UK: Routledge.

Vygotsky, L. (1978). *Mind in society: The development of higher psychological processes.* Cambridge, MA: Harvard University Press.

Warburton, T. (1998). Cartoons and teachers: Mediated visual images as data. In J. Prosser (Ed.), *Image-based research: A sourcebook for qualitative researchers* (pp. 252–262). London, UK: Routledge.

Warburton, T., & Saunders, M. (1996). Representing teachers' professional culture through cartoons. *British Journal of Educational Studies*, *44*(3), 307–325.
Weber, S., & Mitchell, C. (1995). *That's funny, you don't look like a teacher*. London, UK: Falmer Press.
Wetton, N., & McWhirter, J. (1998). Images and curriculum development in health education. In J. Prosser (Ed.), *Image-based research* (pp. 263–283). London, UK: Falmer Press.

5 "Taking It Personally"

Advenience as Reflexivity in Multimodal Research

Throughout this book, I have called attention to multimodality as an emerging and multidisciplinary field that needs to draw on a wide range of different disciplines both theoretically and methodologically (van Leeuwen, 2011). As a researcher engaged in multimodal research in a range of contexts, countries, and communities, I turn to diverse perspectives such as social semiotics, sociocultural approaches, New Literacy Studies, new literacies, visual methodologies, ethnography, and visual anthropology. Understanding how these different disciplines interact, how they are best combined, and how analysis should proceed are still relatively new enterprises in multimodal research, and there is considerable room for new developments and applications (van Leeuwen, 2011). These new enterprises will require "moments of self-reflection" (van Leeuwen, 2011, p. 679) and an accounting for the diverse ways we make and take meaning through overlapping and multiple modes of representation, including our own performances in them (Byrd Clark & Dervin, 2014). In this chapter, I take up the challenge of self-reflection (reflexivity) in multimodal ethnographic research by drawing on Barthes's (1980) concept of "advenience" (i.e., an image's element of disharmony) to situate myself in the analysis of child-created multimodal texts.

In the field of anthropology in general, and ethnography in particular, the "reflexive turn of the 1990s . . . stressed the inseparability of personal from professional identities and the importance of autobiography and personal experience in the production of ethnographic knowledge (Pink, 2013, p. 42). Pink argues that the same point is also of relevance to ethnographers who work with visual images. She argues that we need to "turn the lens" onto ourselves as ethnographic researchers to develop a reflexive awareness of how we use and consume photographs, images, video, online practices, and the like. We need, in other words, "strategies of looking" (Lyon, 2013, p. 25) that account for how ways of seeing are tangled together with intentionalities and subjectivities, including the theories that inform how we make and take meaning as well as the range of relationships represented in visual images and other kinds of multimodal texts across sites of meaning-making, from creator to subject to viewer. Byrd Clark and Dervin (2014) make the case that self-reflection and reflexivity need to be "critical," multifaceted, complex, and ongoing dialogical processes because they are socially situated yet always in motion. Byrd Clark, Mady, and Vanthuyne (2014) note that the "critical" has all too often focused on the outside world rather than questioning one's own beliefs, subjectivities, and strategies. They argue that being critical necessitates "being/becoming aware of one's own performances, experiences, and values, and more importantly, one's investments in such representations" (p. 132). Reflexivity needs to take stock of how we as researchers make meaning through gestures, voice, music, movement, images, and other overlapping modes of representation that call us to invest in particular social meanings and ways of representing. In this chapter, I view reflexivity not as the need to control my biases but rather as the need to acknowledge my positionings, values, and experiences in the interpretive process.

In reflecting on the experiences, representations, power issues, and positionings that I bring to the research process, I take as a starting point Claudia Mitchell's (2011) advice in *Doing Visual Research*. She emphasizes that visual research (or, as I argue here, multimodal research) needs to be taken personally. Taking it personally has "an obvious link to the nature of participatory visual research, in relation to both the researcher and the participants, and in relation to reflexivity as a critical feature of visual research" (p. 5). Gillian Rose in her book *Visual Methodologies*, also suggests that personal engagement with visual images should be the driving force of analysis:

> The most exciting, startling and perceptive critics of visual images don't in the end depend entirely on a sound methodology. . . . They also depend on the pleasure . . . thrills, fascination, wonder, fear, or revulsion of the person looking at the images and then writing about them. Successful interpretation depends on a passionate engagement with what you see. Use your methodology to discipline your passion, not to deaden it.
>
> (2001, p. 4).

I bring the ideas of "taking it personally" and "passionate engagement" together with Barthes's concept of advenience from his reflections on photography in *Camera Lucida*; he writes, "If I like a photograph, if it disturbs me, I linger over it. What am I doing the whole time I remain with it? I look at it. I scrutinize it, as if I wanted to know more about the thing or person it represents" (1980, p. 99). It is worth noting here that a "camera lucida" is an optical device used as a drawing aid by artists; it is tool that renders new ways of seeing and ways of changing the picture by bringing together both what we see and what we imagine. According to Barthes, "in order to see a photograph well, it is best to look away or close your eyes," to bring objects, people, and places into closer view in your mind's eye. Kuhn similarly indicates that interpreting images requires looking away from them: "in order to show what it is evidence of a photograph [image] must always point you away from itself" (1996, p. 474). For Barthes, objects and people in photographs "drift between the shores of perception, between sign and image, without ever approaching either" (p. 20). In other words, it is not the "literal" that provides interest or meaning in an image, but rather, it is the viewer's personal experience, both physical and emotional, of encountering particular images; it is a certain "other" perspective that exerts a sensation (Rowell, 2011) and that is personally touching.

Barthes (1980) elaborates on what he means by "interest" in reflections on his experience looking at photographs in an illustrated magazine. In one example, he describes a photograph of a rebellion in Nicaragua: a street that has been destroyed, two soldiers on patrol, and two nuns in the background. As he explains, his attraction to this image is derived from "the co-presence of two discontinuous elements" that are not seen to belong to the same world: the soldiers and the nuns. In another example, he describes a torn-up road and a child's corpse hidden under a white sheet with parents and friends collected around it. Here, there is also the presence of discontinuities or disharmonies: The corpse has one bare foot; there is a second sheet being carried by the weeping mother. In both of these examples, a duality exists, that is, "an internal agitation . . . the pressure of the unspeakable which wants to be spoken" (Barthes, 1980, p. 19). The images themselves are in no way animated, but how they animate the viewer is what he refers to as the "*advenience* or even *adventure*" (p. 19) of an image.

The two discontinuous elements in advening images are the "studium" and the "punctum." The studium is a special acuity based on human interest in an object (image). It is a kind of special enthusiastic commitment by which the viewer comes to know the producer, the essence of which is the experience of viewing. These are meanings that can be named, have cultural significance, and are broadly understood. The second element is what breaks or disturbs (punctuates) the studium—it rises from the visual scene and "pierces" the viewer. The punctum, however quick, has the power of expansion. It is "that accident which pricks me (but also bruises me, is poignant to me)" (Barthes, 1980, p. 27). This disharmony between the studium and the punctum has been referred to as conscious and unconscious worlds trying to occupy the same space (Rowell, 2011). This is the *advenience* of an image (but not all images will advene) (Barthes, 1980).

In this chapter, I experiment with the concept of advenience as a means of reflexivity in multimodal research by reflecting on what attracts me or touches me personally in certain child-created multimodal texts. The selected texts include photographs but, unlike Barthes, also extend to drawings. I look at these images as Barthes looked at photographs for what advenes, attempting to articulate what it is about these particular images that implicate my own values, interests, experiences, and positionings in the interpretive process. These advening images are "telling cases" (Sheridan, Street, & Bloome, 2000) that I use to surface my own performance in multimodal data analysis. The images are taken from four examples in which participants were engaged in using the visual as both a means of inquiry and representation. The first vignette features a boy's "unknown" image of literacy. The second vignette focuses on home photographs highlighting literacy tools and community identity positionings now and in the future. The third vignette gives prominence to a young boy's "scribble" drawings. In the final vignette, I reflect on the use of an ornate flower as a metaphor in HIV/AIDS billboard posters. Advenience is "an adventuresome adding of a new perspective to the whole" (Johnson, 2005, n.p.), and taken up as researcher reflexivity in interpreting the selected images, I see it as generative and expansive in the interpretive process.

All images represent a complex and recursive relationship among producer, image, and viewer. Rose's (2001) visual methodology, which delineates three interlocking sites of meaning-making (sites of production, image, and viewing) frames the analysis and presentation of the examples. Her framework, as illustrated in Chapter 4, helps make visible the complex recursive producer–image–viewer relationship and foregrounds strands of the multimodal context. At the site of production, I focus on who the participants are and the social, cultural, and historical contexts in which their images are produced. The site of the image itself identifies the content of the image and the possible cultural meanings (studium). The site of viewing is a search for pattern and meaning linked both to how the producer has positioned me to "see" as a viewer and how I experience the viewing (punctum). By focusing on the disharmony between the studium and the punctum, I describe what advenes for me as a researcher and what creates disharmony within an image or when an image is considered within a particular context of research. This concept anchors my analysis and serves to raise questions about the images from my perspective as researcher. I see the sites of meaning-making as recursively relational to each other and the image as one part of a multimodal texture (Norris, 2005) that weaves together different aspects of the participants' lives with my own life, foregrounding and backgrounding various identities, experiences, and positionings across sites of meaning-making.

VIGNETTE 1: DUSTIN'S IMAGE OF LITERACY[1]

This first text was collected as part of a larger study investigating children's "images of literacy." The study, which included students in Grades 1 to 6 (n = 157), took place in a school located in a middle socioeconomic, working-class neighbourhood in one of Canada's western provinces. The focus of the research was on understanding what students' visual depictions of literacy might reveal about the literacy narratives they bring to school and use to make sense of reading and writing.

Sites of Production and Image

The participants initially met in groups for 60 minutes to discuss their ideas and draw pictures about literacy in their lives in school, outside school, and in the future. The groups ranged in size from 4 to 24, with 17 as the average size. They met in grade groups with two researchers (Kendrick and McKay) in the art room of the school, where they were provided with blank white paper, markers, crayons, and pencils. We used guiding questions to shape both the discussion and drawing task: (a) What kind of reading or writing do you do in school or outside of school? (b) Why do you read or write in school or outside of school? (c) Where do you read or write in school or outside of school? (d) How is reading or writing in school both similar and different from reading or writing outside of school? (e) How do you think you will use reading or writing in the future as you grow older? (f) Draw a picture of reading or writing. It can be a picture of reading or writing that you do at home or at school. It can be a picture of reading or writing that you do now or that you think you might do when you're older. The directions for the drawing task were deliberately left open-ended and did not specify who or what should be in the drawing or where it might take place. Students also were asked to create interpretive writing or talk that reflects their own meaning-making process. In other words, units of analysis included both the "primary [immediate] text," the drawings, and the "production text," that is, how the participants engaged in the process of talking and writing about their work (Fiske, 1991).

Data analysis began with broad categorization of the drawings as primary, secondary, or "unknown" images of literacy. Primary images included drawings in which literacy was the central topic of the drawing (e.g., a picture of someone reading books, writing stories and letters, or teaching the alphabet), and secondary images included drawings in which literacy artifacts or events were merely add-ons and not the central topic of the drawing (e.g., a drawing predominantly about dinosaurs but including a small sketch of a book in the corner of the page). Unknown images were much more an anomaly and included drawings that initially did not appear to relate to literacy (e.g., drawings of sports equipment or animals). Our first response was to attribute such "images of literacy" to difficulties understanding the task, more general challenges with reading and writing, or an overall disinterest. In re-examining the 32 drawings in the Grade 5 collection, however, I became particularly engaged with one of the "unknown" images, which was significantly different from others in this category that mostly included solitary pieces of sports equipment such as a baseball, a football, or a hockey stick. This image was of a boy, rifle in hand, standing beside a freshly killed buck (see Figure 5.1). This was Dustin's (age 11) drawing: In it, he makes direct eye contact with the viewer. His facial expression and bodily stance communicate visible pride in his accomplishment, corroborated by his explanation on the front of the drawing: "I shot my first buck with a doble [sic] barel shotgut [sic]. It is at my grapernts [sic] farm. My dad helped me."

At the outset of the project, Dustin sauntered into the art room with considerable confidence; he appeared to be a leader among his peers. During the production of the drawing, he enjoyed making witty remarks to attract attention, especially that of his peers. He was very engaged in the drawing activity yet mysteriously kept his work cloaked in secrecy. His first

Figure 5.1 "My First Buck"

drawing—curiously of a gopher being shot—was shown to only a select few boys, who spoke in hushed tones as they pored over the drawing. Dustin eventually crumpled this drawing into a ball, obscuring it from our view. Prior to his second drawing attempt, he sought clarification about the assignment: "Can we draw anything we want about reading and writing?" "Does our teacher get to see it?" Once reassured that he was free to draw what he chose, and that his teacher would not see the drawing without his permission, he set to work with quiet determination.

Site of Viewing

The primary audience for this image was literacy researchers, but a secondary audience was Dustin's peers as part of the context and process. What advenes for me in this image is the disharmony between my own notions of literacy (e.g., as connected to reading and writing practices) and the image of a freshly killed animal. The image evokes memories from my own childhood, having grown up in a context similar to Dustin's. I am reminded of my father's fall hunting trips in Alberta and the first experience of peering through the living room window to see, with both horror and intrigue, a deer or elk hanging from a winch on the back of a truck. Despite my own experience, I struggled to connect hunting with literacy and wondered what the experience might mean to Dustin. I had questions about the secrecy surrounding the production of this particular drawing within the school context. These questions created considerable interest in this unusual image, and we set out to find out more through an interview with Dustin.

During the interview, Dustin was serious, cooperative, and articulate. He began by listing his favorite pastimes: "playing hockey, rollerblading, and basketball." He identified "gym" as his preferred subject in school "because it's the most fun." This partiality for action appeared again when we asked him about what he liked to read and write. "Sometimes I read books," he explained. "It depends if I want to learn more about something. Like, I'd probably read about hockey." Additional reading interests included Harry Potter and "a book about the fur trade and Samuel D. Champlain's Indians and stuff." Dustin explained that he would rather watch a story on television than read it because "instead of just reading about, you can see the action while you're watching, and you can hear exactly what they're saying and stuff." Despite his inclination to watch television, he indicated that he spent up to two hours reading at home every day, although he confessed that most of his reading related to homework. Although he explained that he did sometimes read his own books at home, he was uncertain about how many books he owned. He sometimes borrowed books from the public library. When asked how he felt about reading, Dustin responded, "The stuff I like is pretty good. But sometimes, instead of just reading a book, I take the dictionary out and try to find stuff." He was somewhat less enthusiastic about writing, explaining, "I like writing some stuff 'cause last year I wanted to make up my own little stories, but then I wrote two chapters of it, then I never had enough time." Further discussion about school writing tasks was particularly revealing in relation to the image of literacy he created:

Maureen: What about when you write? What do you think about?

Dustin: When I write, I sometimes think about if I could write and then what I would write. Like, I think about what I wanna write if I can.

Maureen: Do you mean it's hard for you to get your ideas down on paper?

Dustin: Yeah, 'cause I'm thinking about something else that I *wanna* put down, but we're not allowed.

Maureen: Can you tell me more about that?

Dustin: Like, sometimes when she [the teacher], say, she writes, "What did you do on the weekend?" I wanna write like I was shooting gophers or something like that. We're not allowed to write about anything with violence.

Maureen: So, if you were allowed to write about those kinds of topics, how would that help you as a writer?

Dustin: I would probably get better marks [because it would be about] things I'm interested in and stuff I know about.

Maureen: When you first drew your picture, you drew a gopher before, right? What were you thinking about when you drew that picture?

Dustin: Sometimes I write about what I want to do in the future and stuff, and I think about that, and I draw and write about what I did already. Like it might be something that happened four years ago, I draw about that, if I remember it and it was good.

Maureen: So when you're asked to write about things in school, do you sometimes find it hard to write about what the teacher asks you to write about?

Dustin: Yeah, she just wants us to write about sunny days and stuff like that.

A follow-up interview with Dustin's teacher confirmed that guns, blood, and dismemberment were banned from classroom drawing, writing, and reading as part of the school's "zero tolerance" policy on violence, a policy that was at the time common in many schools in the district because of the Columbine High School massacre in 1999 (see, e.g., https://en.wikipedia.org/wiki/Columbine_High_School_massacre) and widespread fear that students might act on the violence they wrote about. His position on his school's policy also was evident in his blank journal: When he was told on the Monday mornings following his weekend hunting trips with his father and grandfather to write about his weekend, he sat in silent resistance.

By attending to the advenience of Dustin's image—the disharmony between my own notions of what literacy is and the image this student created—a powerful image of literacy emerges, an image of what Dustin was not allowed to write about in his classroom. As he so poignantly explained, "She [the teacher] just wants us to write about sunny days and stuff like that." Because visually communicated information can be much more easily denied and dismissed as being "in the eye of the beholder" (van Leeuwen, 2000, p. 335), Dustin was able to use this mode of communication as a safety zone that allowed him to bring into the classroom life experiences that may not meet with his teacher's approval but also to take a personal stand on his school's no violence policy. His positioning directs us to look away from the image toward his resistance as a writer in the classroom.

VIGNETTE 2: CARL'S SELF-PORTRAITS[2]

This second vignette is taken from a larger research project that used Ewald's Literacy Through Photography approach (see Ewald & Lightfoot, 2002) to engage a group of Grades 6 and 7 students in taking still photos (primary texts) and writing narratives (production texts) (Fiske, 1991) in relation to four themes: self, school, community, and dreams. The students who participated in this project attended an elementary school in an inner-city community in a western Canadian city. Their school was featured in a Canadian documentary programme on inner-city education. The documentary portrayed the "dark side" of this community, directing the viewers' attention to images that related to "drugs, gangs, and prostitution" in conjunction with social issues labeled as "illiteracy, poverty, and family dysfunction." The multimodal project was intended to provide an opportunity for students to speak back to the media by producing their own narratives about their school, their community, and ultimately, themselves. Both visual and linguistic modes were used as narrative resources that allowed students to situate themselves uniquely within the context of their school and community.

Site of Production

At the outset of the project, students received training in photographic methods and participated in a range of discussions during a school-based workshop that included a professional photographer and art educator (Mike Emme). The students, many of whom had never held a camera, were provided with disposable cameras and encouraged to produce a collection of 24 photographs. After the photographs were developed, the students wrote in a journal about their images (e.g., why they took the photo and what it meant to them). Students had the opportunity to display their photographs and narratives in a variety of combinations (as single images, images and text, image sequences, or a slide show with audio) and contexts (in class, with caregivers and friends, and with the larger community, including media personnel). These multiple readings allowed students to explore their own identities and the range of ways identity can be constructed through visual texts.

Sites of Image and Viewing

In response to the invitation to photograph their lives at school, at home, and in the community, students produced a range of images that captured their sense of pride in their school and their community; the importance of relationships with family, friends, and teachers; and childhood memories evoked by places and objects captured on film. One set of images, however, stood apart from the others because they offered a glimpse into the future. These images were created by Carl (age 12) in the context of his home and community.

In this first image, Carl is sitting at his desk in his bedroom "on the weekend" (see Figure 5.2). He is dressed casually in a T-shirt and jeans, writing in a notebook. On the left side of the desk is a collection of small plants. On the right corner is a stack of books, an English Oxford dictionary prominently set on top. In his journal, Carl writes: "This picture shows how hard I work . . . an ordinary Gr. 7 boy in his classroom . . . smiling like an idiot." I find his use of the word *ordinary* compelling here, given that it was only two years prior to this project that he first started learning English. As a Grade 7 student, he emerged as one of the strongest all-round students, academically, socially and athletically.

Figure 5.2 Carl Hard at Work

Carl juxtaposed this first image with a second photograph of himself, similarly seated at a desk in his home but this time in front of a computer (see Figure 5.3), dressed in a shirt and tie. As Carl described in his journal, "A business guy sitting on a computer all day long trying to be Bill Gates . . . I think this is what I will be when I grow up." Together, the images show Carl's identity across time and space, from hard-working student studying English to wealthy businessman using a computer. He has a vision of what success means to him, what it looks like, and what attributes and tools are necessary to achieve it. When his visual texts are situated within the context of the media's portrayal of his school and community, a sharp contrast is evident. My attraction to these two images isn't derived from the images themselves, but rather, the attraction comes from "looking away"—a process that evokes other images of objects, people, and places that can expand the interpretation (Barthes, 1980). What becomes visible is Carl's powerful sense of hope for himself and the future of his community. As a child living in an under-resourced community, he imagines a future identity

Figure 5.3 Carl as a Businessman

that transcends those of drug dealer, gang member, and sex trade worker, identities that dominated in the media portrayal of this community. As Carl further explained in his journal,

> I don't think it was very nice to say our school is poor and everything. We are kids and it discourages us to say that we are poor. . . . It hurts us to hear that we are one of the poorest communities. . . . It is filled with drug dealers, prostitutes and homeless people. But our school has tried to make us feel safe. . . . Don't judge us by this community. We are just kids and we do not deserve to hear bad things about us at this age.

Thus, the two images taken literally are not what advene for me, but rather, it is what underpins them. Specifically, when I situate the images in the context of the media, while simultaneously looking away from the literal content of the images, what becomes visible is a sense of hope both for this boy and the future of his community, a sentiment that is in sharp contrast to the media's portrayal. The visual allowed Carl to speak back to the media by showing a counter-identity imbued with his own values, hopes, and dreams. He was able to reposition his own identity to make visible who *he* imagines he can become in this community. His compositional choices in the photographs constitute what Willis (1977) refers to as "the organization of self in relation to the future" (p. 172). The meanings reflect reality as imagined by this sign-maker, influenced by his beliefs, values, and biases. Norton (2000) contends that students' imagined identities and communities provide a key to understanding how and why they engage or do not engage with particular literacy practices (such as those associated with a hard-working student, as in Carl's case). It is only by "looking away" from this image that other objects, people, and places come into view, thereby expanding my interpretation of the literal content of the images.

VIGNETTE 3: NOLAN'S "SCRIBBLE" DRAWINGS

This third vignette showcases a series of "scribble" drawings created by a 4.5-year-old boy. The images were part of my ongoing documentation of my own son's early attempts at communicating and representing his ideas through multiple modes. As a young child, he had a passion for action. His preference was to use language, movement, or gestures to represent ideas and concepts. Although paper, writing, and art tools were regularly accessible to him, his interest in two-dimensional form was typically limited to colouring sheets or, on some occasions, painting or writing letters of the alphabet and practicing his name. During the summer he was four, I began to find what looked like "scribble drawings" that were at first glance difficult to make sense of because the scribble tended to mask the object or figure underneath.

Sites of Production and Image

This first series of drawings was created in a hotel room where we were staying while on summer holidays. Nolan drew each image on a separate piece of paper—all were still attached to a small pad of hotel notepaper that he found

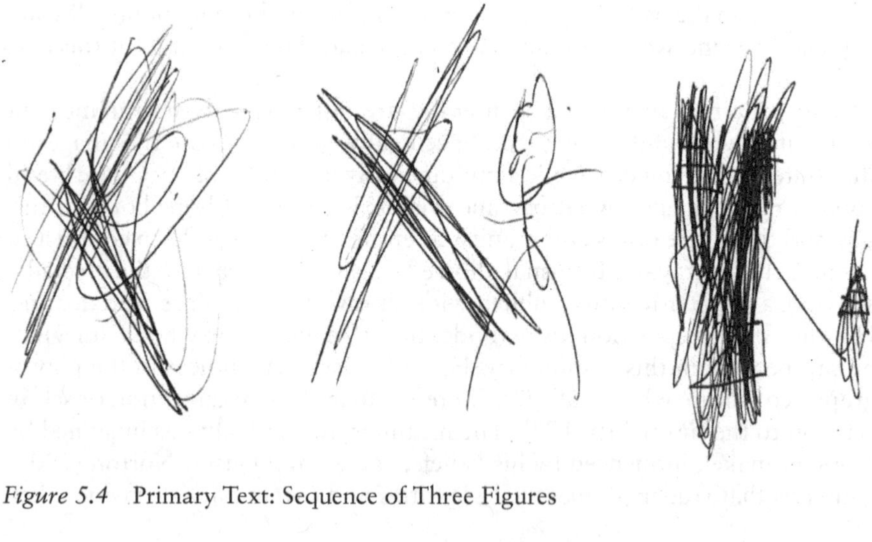

Figure 5.4 Primary Text: Sequence of Three Figures

on the desk in our room. Each drawing in the series of three appears to have a figure that has been scratched out or scribbled over. Only the second image appears to have one figure (on the right side) that is visible. The third image has a figure, although possibly more detailed, obscured by a heavier scribble.

Site of Viewing and Site of New Production

When I first started to discover these types of drawings in Nolan's paper-and-pencil creations, I was, on the one hand, pleased to know that he was experimenting with drawing and that the frequency of creation was increasing. I was at the same time concerned, however, that his drawings may somehow not be meeting his own expectations for what objects should look like in two-dimensional form. Each image was similar—a figure or object scratched out, scribbled over, or obscured from view. I couldn't help but wonder why. This was what initially attracted me to the images: the scribble that disturbed and masked the underlying scene. What was happening here?

Initially, I tried to understand each of the "scribble" drawings as a finished product. It wasn't until I observed Nolan's process that my interpretation shifted. Figure 5.5 shows a somewhat different version of the figures and scribbles theme evident in the other drawings. In the centre of the children's menu (from the restaurant in our hotel) are two visible yellow figures joined by a scribble where their hands and arms meet. The figures are simple in form

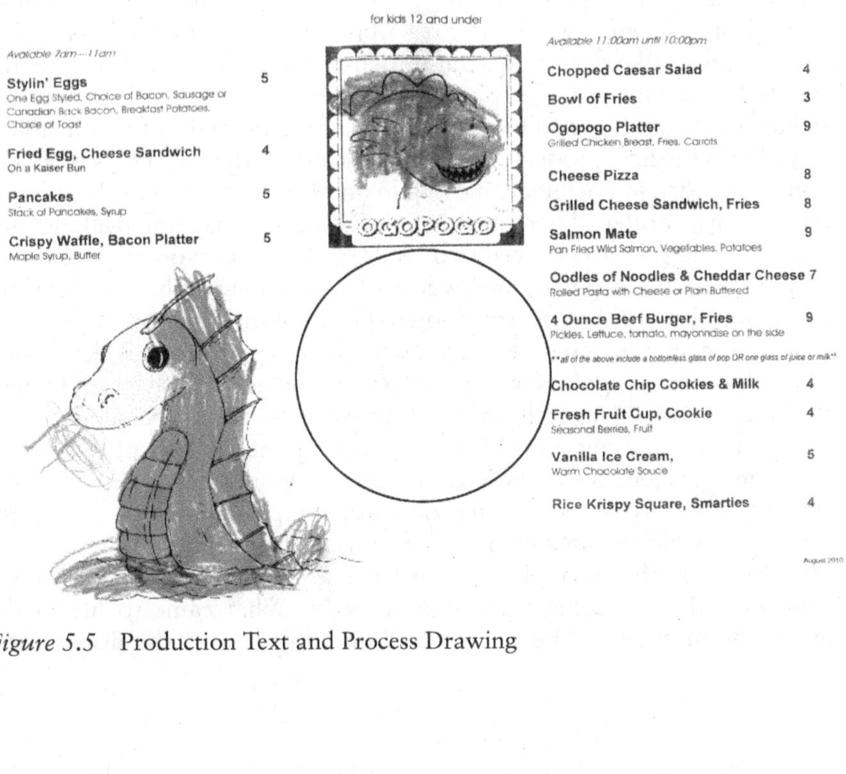

Figure 5.5 Production Text and Process Drawing

with little detail but nonetheless visible (i.e., not masked by the scribble). Here, he took two ends of a broken crayon, one in each hand. The figures were drawn with both hands operating in tandem. Once the figures were complete, the crayons became fighting implements (swords perhaps), with his hands serving as an extension of the figures so that he could act out a battle. The scribble shows traces of the conflict. What seems to be of interest to the sign-maker here is the action itself rather than the drawing as product; the process is what engages, and the drawing serves no purpose after the battle. Here, the visual outcome masks the action and complex thinking that took place as the drawing was being created (see also Wohlwend, 2010).

A re-examination of the first series of three "scribble" drawings shows traces of "battles." In the first image, the figure beneath the scribble has been obliterated in the fight ("killed by a bomb" I am told when I ask). In the second, the victor appears on the right side, having obscured the opponent on the left. The same is evident in the third drawing, though the victor is somewhat smaller. In all of the frames, the interests of the sign-maker and meaning of the images are not initially evident. It was only by witnessing the producer's process that meaning became evident; here, interest is in action, specifically acting out rather than simply representing a battle scene in two-dimensional form. As Kress argues, when the representation "comes off the page," it enters another world (1997, p. 25). It moves from contemplation on the page to action in the here and now. While it is on the page, the maker can do mental things with it. It is a mental object, distant, and accessible by sight and imagination in the world of the page. When the object is off the page, the maker can engage in "physical" action-oriented things. Unlike the example Kress provides, however, where objects when cut from paper become real objects accessible by touch as well as sight, the objects (the figures) remain in two-dimensional form. It is only the action itself that comes off the page and becomes located somewhere between two-dimensional and three-dimensional form. The only trace of that action is the scribble in the final product. Kress points out that when the limits of imagination are reached in one mode, moving to another mode extends those limits in certain ways or offers different potential. Cutting out may offer children one means of bridging a gap between two kinds of imaginary worlds—one where the child enters the page and one where objects come off the page and are brought into the world of physical objects. By exploring in more depth what advenes for me in this series of images, what becomes apparent is that action can be suspended along this continuum between things on the page and things in the here and now. This realization reveals meaning-making possibilities that I had not previously considered but that were an integral part of this child's meaning-making repertoire. As Kress observes, the analytical eyes of young sign-makers quickly assess the meaning-making possibilities of the world around them, which is fused with a mental image of context.

Advenience in this example is the disharmony between the primary texts or images and the production text or process. What came to life in the process was masked by the image itself. By attending to the disharmony between image and production, I was able to open up the interpretive process in a way that would not have been possible had I worked with the image alone and had I not incorporated my own personal response, which served to generate new questions about what the image might mean or represent.

VIGNETTE 4: ROSALEE'S HIV/AIDS BILLBOARD POSTER

This final vignette was part of a larger study focusing on cultural practices and HIV/AIDS health literacy in Uganda. Participants included 100 students in Grades 3 through 7. The students attend a residential primary school in Uganda's Central Region. The school was opened following the establishment of one of Uganda's new universities to accommodate the children of university staff as well as children from other districts in Uganda and beyond as far as Tanzania, Kenya, and Rwanda. The school is comprised of modern buildings and facilities arranged to form quadrangles with dormitories, classes, and the administration offices arranged in blocks. The student population includes a diverse linguistic and culturally mixed gender groups with a range of experiences and health literacy knowledge related to HIV/AIDS.

Site of Production

Students' knowledge and perceptions of cultural practices and the spread of HIV/AIDS were elicited as part of a class discussion. HIV/AIDS education is a required curriculum topic in all schools, and students are exposed to various public service announcements on radio and television, as billboards, and in various other modes as part of a national campaign to prevent HIV/AIDS. Students viewed and discussed their interpretations of billboards designed to sensitize people to the dangers of HIV/AIDS. Using selected photographs of billboards from their own community and those from other countries in Africa, students were asked to share their knowledge, experience, and interpretations of the billboards and what messages they drew from them. A projector and screen were used to enable the students to view the billboards in a large format and to discuss each one. During the discussion, students were asked the following questions:

1. What message do you get from this billboard?
2. Other than what is written on this billboard, what else do you learn from it (e.g., from the images)?
3. What does this billboard teach us?

After discussing a range of billboards, the students were asked to draw their own billboards for HIV/AIDS prevention and include captions or explanations. The students' messages were embedded in the social conditions of their local context, and a number depicted difficult knowledge such as rape and exploitation of children. All the messages portrayed the complexity of intimate human relationships (e.g., child–child, child–adult, and adult–adult) across various contexts and situations. What most captured my interest in a number of the images was the inclusion of an ornate, detailed flower that seemed in disharmony with much of the difficult knowledge students were representing. At times, the flower is floating in the air; in other instances, it is being held or offered. Always, it is situated between two individuals who are depicted as resisting, contemplating, or committing to a sexual relationship.

In a previous study of images of HIV/AIDS (see Chapter 4), we collected cartoon drawings created by secondary school students who used stick figures in black and white rather than full-colour posters such as the one featured in this vignette. Nowhere does a flower appear in any of the cartoon messages, nor have I seen one on actual billboards in Uganda. Yet in this new collection of messages, the primary students use it as their own construction for communicating knowledge and information about HIV/AIDS prevention. What I am drawn to is the subtle, layered, yet powerful use of this sign.

Site of Image and Site of Viewing

Rosalee's billboard message is the focus of this final vignette (see Figure 5.6). In the left frame, a male figure is offering a female figure a small, black flower; the flower is being offered as a gift, which in this context is a way of

Figure 5.6 Rosalee's HIV/AIDS Billboard

declaring one's love (or the promise of love) for another, in this case, with dire consequences as the caption reads, "I give you this flower and I rape you." Below the image, Rosalee has written: "That is the way of getting HIV/AIDS. THIS DISEASE is caused by raping." The positioning of the girl's hands seem to indicate that she is rejecting the offer of the flower, yet her facial expression with its faint smile does not match the gesture. The expression is subtle, and its juxtaposition with the hand gestures reveals the female figure's dilemma, which is possibly a temptation to accept the flower. Although she may fear the stated consequences, that taking the flower will result in rape, like many young girls who live in poverty and whose families cannot afford school fees or other material possessions, she also may be tempted by gifts. This dilemma indexes the social issue of "sugar daddies," who all too commonly lure young girls through the promise of love and material goods. Knowing the short lifespan of picked flowers, the girl may on the one hand fully understand the fleeting promise of the flower as the kind of love that will be short lived, particularly in the shadow of sexual assault and HIV/AIDS.

In contrast, in the second frame the caption reads: "HUSBAND AND WIFE AS A MAN AND WOMAN." A larger, yellow flower appears between the two figures, and they are both touching it with their outstretched hands. The size here can be compared to that in the first frame as potentially representing love that is longer lasting and more enduring, although still fragile. Interestingly, although the woman's hands are touching the flower, her gesture is similar to the female figure in the left frame, where the flower is being pushed away. The message here also is mixed, and it raises the question of whether the woman foresees the inherent danger of engaging in any sexual relationship, even marriage. Since the all-time low of 6.4 percent in 2006, HIV prevalence has been on the rise in Uganda, with 150,000 new infections diagnosed each year (20,600 are children) and one in five men reporting unfaithfulness (AVERT, 2015). Rosalee's choice to represent a female perspective in her message also addresses current concerns that because Ugandan women typically marry and become sexually active at a younger age than their male counterparts and have older and more sexually experienced partners, they are at an increased risk of contracting HIV (AVERT, 2015).

Taking up advenience as reflexivity is particularly challenging when dealing with difficult knowledge such as sexual assault, unfaithful partners, and the consequences of HIV/AIDS. By attending to Rosalee's imaginative use of a flower in her billboard poster as a point of entry into her message, her layered and conflicting meanings are made more visible. From a reflexivity perspective, it is my own positioning as a woman that locates my interpretation of this message in a particular way; as a woman, I am more invested in the perspectives of women and girls and the issues they face.

ADVENIENCE AS REFLEXIVITY

As noted at the outset of this chapter, being forthcoming about how interpretations arise at all stages of our analysis of multimodal texts is a critical component of advancing research in the emerging field of multimodality. As researchers, we need ways to examine when and how personal experience shapes our interpretation to better understand how our everyday encounters with multimodal texts, in terms of both primary texts and production texts, relate back to our lives, memories, and histories. In each of the vignettes described in this chapter, advenience served as a tool that allowed me as a researcher to "look away" in order to look in at how my own experiences, biases, and assumptions shape the interpretive process. Attending to what advenes in multimodal texts renders new ways of seeing and ways of changing the picture by bringing together both what we see and what we imagine. In this way, the concept of advenience helps "get at" the illusive relationships between producer and viewer. It helps me account for the diverse ways I make and take meaning through overlapping and multiple modes of representation, including my own performances in them.

Qualitative research has in place researcher reflexivity, but this is far less developed in multimodal research. I offer advenience not as an answer but rather a starting point for thinking about how our own life stories are reflected in our research from questions to interpretations. I hope that through the examples in this chapter, I have been able to demonstrate the range of ways in which the concept of advenience can be a means of acknowledging how our own life stories shape our interpretations of multimodal texts. In the case of Dustin, I am directed to look away from the image toward his practice as writer in the classroom. In the second example, the juxtaposition between Carl's self-portraits and the media portrayal of his school and community (so, image in relation to the wider social context) raises questions about Carl's imagined future identity. The disharmony between Nolan's scribble drawings and his production process opens up interpretation in new ways. In all three of these examples, the advenience of the image is at the intersection of the primary text (i.e., the image) and the production text. In the final example, it is the unexpected positioning of a flower against the backdrop of sexual violence that captures my interest. The object is much more than a flower; it is symbolic of the risk of HIV/AIDS in a range of different types of sexual relationships that may involve violence and betrayal. In this example, this disturbing content and difficult knowledge displayed in an image created by an elementary school girl raise questions about the heightened vulnerability of girls and women to HIV/AIDS in this rural context of Uganda.

Taking up the concept of advenience as integral to researcher-as-audience raises important questions about how we engage with and open up the interpretation of multimodal texts, which are accretive, layered constructions of meaning. As researchers, do we engage differently with different modes? Do visual images touch us in a way that is different from words? Does a performative text evoke yet other response affectively, cognitively, or physically? When working with multimodal texts, can we simply apply reflexivity practices that have been developed in qualitative research more generally and language-based research practices in particular (e.g., interviews and written accounts of observation)? Images that are collected as part of literacy and multimodal studies have audiences beyond the researcher. As researchers, how do we address the ethics of what might advene for other audiences viewing difficult content such as rape (see also Chapter 4) in our dissemination of research results, either in journal articles or as part of an installation or exhibition (see Mitchell, 2011, for a discussion of ethics and audiencing for this format)? What are the consequences of writing ourselves into our research as part of reflexivity, specifically in relation to advenience and what touches us personally? Each of the images in this chapter is one part of a "multimodal texture" (Norris, 2005) that weaves together different aspects of the participants' lives with my own life, foregrounding and backgrounding various identities, experiences, and positionings across sites of meaning-making. Mitchell, Theron, Stuart, Smith, and Campbell (2011) argue that as researchers, it is critical to "draw ourselves" into the research (p. 34). Yet, reflexivity can be much more challenging when interpreting representations of violence, sexual or otherwise.

As Mitchell et al. (2011) delineate, there are many points of entry for working with visual images:

> (1) a consideration of what the individual participants themselves say about their [images] (either during interviews or in their captions), (2) an analysis of the shared discussions, (3) a thematic analysis of key issues (with supporting evidence of the drawings and commentary), (4) the responses of audiences at the time of civic dissemination (Who says what? Which images are particularly compelling to community audiences and to broader audiences? Are there thematic aspects that can be explored in audience response?), and of course, what is most desirable, and (5) the triangulation of these various data sources.
>
> (p. 30)

I see advenience as a possible first point of entry, an initial "strategy of looking" (Lyon, 2013, p. 25) at multimodal texts such as visual images. It is a helpful concept for thinking more deeply about how the questions that arise as part of the interpretative process are inextricably linked to our own positionalities, subjectivities, and histories. Reflecting more openly on how we arrive at our research interpretations and how our lives intersect with those of our participants enhances not only our understandings of ourselves, our participants, and the issues we investigate but also the reach and authenticity of our findings.

NOTES

1. An extended version of this case study was published in Kendrick and McKay (2003). I gratefully acknowledge the contributions of Roberta McKay in the work on children's images of literacy.
2. An extended version of this case study was first published in Kendrick and Rowsell (2014).

REFERENCES

AVERT. (2015). HIV & AIDS in Uganda. Retrieved from http://www.avert.org/hiv-aids-uganda.htm

Barthes, R. (1980). *Camera lucida: Reflections on photography*. New York, NY: Hill and Wang.

Byrd Clark, J., & Dervin, F. (2014). Introduction. In J. Byrd Clark & F. Dervin (Eds.), *Reflexivity and multimodality in language education: Rethinking multilingualism and interculturality in accelerating, complex and transnational spaces* (pp. 1–62). London, UK: Routledge.

Byrd Clark, J., Mady, C., & Vanthuyne, A. (2014). Exploring reflexivity and multilingualism in three French language teacher education programs. *Canadian Journal of Applied Linguistics, 17*(1), 129–155.

Ewald, W., & Lightfoot, A. (2002). *I wanna take me a picture: Teaching photography and writing to children*. Boston, MA: Beacon.

Fiske, J. (1991). *Understanding popular culture*. Boston, MA: Unwin.

Johnson, R. (2005). Adventures in advenience: The return of a photographic moment. Retrieved from http://richardalexanderjohnson.com/2012/01/12/adventures-in-advenience-the-return-of-a-photographic-moment-2/

Kendrick, M., & McKay, R. (2003). Revisiting children's images of literacy. *Language & Literacy*, *5*(1), 1–17. Retrieved from http://educ.queensu.ca/~landl/index.htm

Kendrick, M., & Rowsell, J. (2014). The visual turn: Transitioning into visual approaches to literacy education. In S. Elliot-Johns & D. Jarvis (Eds.), *Perspectives on transitions in schooling and instructional practice* (pp. 320–346). Toronto, ON: University of Toronto Press.

Kress, G. (1997). *Before writing: Rethinking the paths to literacy*. London, UK: Routledge.

Kuhn, A. (1996). Remembrance. In L. Heron & V. Williams (Eds.), *Illuminations: Women writing on photography from the 1850s to the present* (pp. 146–161). Durham, NC: Duke University Press.

Lipman, M. (2003). *Thinking in education*. Cambridge, UK: Cambridge University Press.

Lyon, D. (2013). The labour of refurbishment: Space and time, and the building and the body. In S. Pink, D. E. Tutt, & A. Dainty (Eds.), *Ethnographic research in the construction of industry* (pp. 23–39). Oxford, UK: Routledge.

Mitchell, C. (2011). *Doing visual research*. London, UK: Sage.

Mitchell, C., Theron, L, Stuart, J., Smith, A., & Campbell, Z. (2011). Drawings as research method. In L. Theron, C. Mitchell, A. Smith, & J. Stuart (Eds.), *Picturing research: Drawing as visual methodology* (pp. 19–36). Rotterdam, Netherlands: Sense Publishers.

Norris, S. (2005). Habitus, social identity, the perception of male dominations—and agency? In S. Norrris & R. Jones (Eds.), *Discourse in action: Introducing mediated discourse analysis* (pp. 183–198). London, UK: Routledge.

Norton, B. (2000). *Identity and language learning: Gender, ethnicity and educational change*. Harlow, UK: Pearson Education Limited.
Pink, S. (2013). *Doing visual ethnography*. London, UK: Sage.
Rose, G. (2001). *Visual methodologies*. London, UK: Sage.
Rowell, S. (2011). The art of pathography—A thematic analysis of the photographic self-portrait. Paper on: Camera lucida Roland Barthes. Retrieved from http://spencerrowellresearch.blogspot.ca/2011/05/camera-lucida-notes-barthes-r-1980-p.html
Sheridan, D., Street, B., & Bloome, D. (2000). *Writing ourselves: Mass-observation and literacy practices*. Cresskill, NJ: Hampton Press.
van Leeuwen, T. (2011). Multimodality. In J. Simpson (Ed.), *The Routledge handbook of applied linguistics* (pp. 668–682). London, UK: Routledge.
van Leeuwen, T. (2000). Visual racism. In M. Reisigl & R. Wodak (Eds.), *The semiotics of racism: Approaches in critical discourse analysis* (pp. 333–350). Vienna, Austria: Passagen Verlag.
Willis, P. (1977). *Learning to labour: How working class kids get working class jobs*. London, UK: Gower Publishing Company Limited.
Wohlwend, K. (2010). A is for Avatar: Young children in literacy 2.0 worlds and literacy 1.0 schools. *Language Arts, 88*(2), 144–152.

6 Final Thoughts and Perspective

In this final section, I briefly review key findings from each of the chapters with an eye to future directions for research and pedagogy in the area of literacy and multimodality. I begin by highlighting influential themes from each of the chapters.

In Chapter 1, I argue that because synaesthetic activity is a natural part of imaginative play, it enables learners to seamlessly shift across modes and languages in a low-risk context. This movement has considerable potential for supporting the development of young learners' semiotic repertoires, including their metacognitive, meta/cross-linguistic, and meta-modal awareness. Moreover, by engaging with young learners in the play activities they initiate, educators and researchers can develop a more intimate and detailed understanding of what is happening as children make meaning through multiple languages, modes, and identities. These complex multimodal ensembles that children create in play are at the heart of what it means to be both imaginative and creative.

Chapter 2's focus on play also highlights the intimate connection between play and multimodality through additional examples that move beyond early childhood. By better understanding the symbiosis between play and multimodality, it may be possible to see new avenues for the development of learning theories and pedagogical practices from early childhood to adulthood. Because play offers all learners a protected space for experimentation with different modes and communicative practices, it provides unique and important opportunities for them to engage in performance before competence (Cazden, 1981). As individuals select modes, identities, and narratives that suit their individual learning purposes and communicative needs, they offer glimpses of authentic lives and communities. Where these lives and experiences have not been well represented in classrooms or in the research literature, new possibilities are presented.

In Chapter 3, I advocate for using the visual to understand how children conceptualize complex concepts such as literacy. This position aligns with van Leeuwen's (2015) recent argument that the new agenda for educators must include "the specific visual literacies of school subjects and domains of institutional practice, and seek to ensure that these form part of teacher education at a high level" (pp. 587–588). This agenda also needs to consider the visual in terms of communicative practices more broadly rather than continuing to frame studies of the visual simply on the need to understand literacy (Yamada-Rice, 2015), which tend to perpetuate the privileging of written modes of communication in classroom contexts.

Similarly, Chapter 4 makes the case that we need to think of literacy studies more broadly in terms of *multimodal studies*, which sets as an agenda investigating all communicative practices as multimodal ensembles but also carefully considering the particular range of semiotic modes that have been given value in a culture. As Kress (2015) points out,

> Certain modes may not exist in some communities . . . for a variety of reasons. Across the world, many communities had not and still have not developed the resource of making marks on surfaces into *writing* as mode. And certainly, this possibility has been developed very differently, as is evident in deeply differing script systems, or evident in the purposes for which that material/semiotic resource has been used, in the recording of culturally significant factors—historical, economic, mythic, or other. If a mode is "missing" (by comparison with another community) it may be because it had not been essential for the effective working of that community. (p. 56)

Chapter 5 stresses that new modes of data collection require new means of analysis, integral to which are researcher reflexivity and attention to how we interact with various modes, in particular the visual. Specifically, I use Barthes's (1980) concept of advenience to think more deeply about the interconnections between the questions that arise as part of the interpretative process and our own positionalities, subjectivities, and histories as researchers.

NEW DIRECTIONS

Within and across the five chapters, I have put data examples from diverse projects in conversation with each other, and in the process, some directions and questions for further research emerge. Interwoven with these new directions are two core presuppositions: (1) Play is the ultimate multimodal context. Drawing attention to play as a communicative practice not only in early childhood but well beyond holds promise for significantly advancing our understanding of how multiple modes interact and build on one another. And (2) thinking takes place in all modes, not just in language. Harnessing this awareness in research and teaching across diverse contexts would expand possibilities for understanding the lives and experiences of others. The new directions that I briefly describe next bring together these two central themes with a more specific focus on cross-cultural studies, funds of knowledge, inquiry-based learning, and creativity.

1. **A cross-cultural turn:** In writing this book, I wanted to draw attention to how multimodality works in a range of contexts—not just "Western" contexts—and its potential for creating access to new knowledge and new opportunities. Advancing studies in multimodality requires maintaining a strong focus on cross-cultural research. This cross-cultural turn has the potential to open up new understandings about the uses and purposes of multimodal practices, including how various modes work in different cultures (as was the case with literacy studies in the past). As Kress notes, "valuations of semiotic resources are bound to be different in different communities. The social / cultural / semiotic world of every community depends on how the senses have been and are valued, fostered, developed in a community" (2015, p. 56). A subfocus of the new direction needs to consider more carefully the relationship between multilingualism and multimodality, an area that has not been systematically studied (see Early, Kendrick, & Potts, 2015).
2. **Modes as funds of knowledge:** The concept of "funds of knowledge" has been used to describe the *intellectual resources* of minority language groups (see Moll & Greenberg, 1990). In the introductory chapter of this book, I position "multimodal ways of knowing" as intellectual resources. Reconsidering funds of knowledge from a social semiotic perspective recognizes that cognition takes place in all modes and all languages. All funds of knowledge are intellectual resources that when studied in detail, have the potential to expand our understanding of how individuals across communities make meaning in the world. As Kress vehemently argues, social semiotics "is a theory which insists that semiotic work—work done by everyone, constantly, everywhere—be accorded recognition" (2015, p. 69).
3. **Inquiry-based learning:** An emerging trend in both teacher education and curriculum and pedagogy is the resurgence of inquiry-based teaching and learning. Inquiry-based learning has been discussed widely for many years (Harpaz, 2005; Harpaz & Lefstein, 2000; Kuhlthau, Maniotes, & Caspari, 2007; Lipman, 2003; McTighe & Wiggins, 2013; Shanahan, 1997; Wiggins & McTighe, 2005). Dewey's (1958) ideas have been very influential in this area, including his notion of teacher as artist and scientist, and art as problem-solving behaviour. For example, in 2009, Brickman, Gormally, Armstrong, and Hallar observed that there had been "decades" of policy statements in the United States attempting to define inquiry-based teaching and learning; one of its many meanings was the provision of learning activities in science education that were modelled on the practices of real scientists. In other subject areas, inquiry learning has been described as a method by which "students learn content as well as discipline-specific reasoning skills and practices . . . by collaboratively engaging in investigations" (Hmelo-Silver, Duncan, Clark, & Chinn, 2007, p. 100). There is also a large body of literature that describes using inquiry learning in different subject areas. Yet, recognition that because students think in

different modes, they need opportunities to inquire in different modes (e.g., via the visual, the audio, the kinaesthetic, etc.), has not been well articulated in this literature. The renewed popularity of inquiry-based learning needs to take seriously the importance of cognition, and hence inquiry, taking place in all modes, not just in language. Investigating the possibilities of inquiry-based learning from a social semiotic perspective has considerable potential for researchers, teachers, and learners.

4. **Play, multimodality, and creativity:** Similar to inquiry-based learning, much has been written in education about creativity, particularly from a cognitive perspective. Creative activity as part of play has always been one of the cornerstones of early childhood education, yet it has been emphasized much less in the older grades. Multimodal activities such as play-, art-, and discovery-based learning are generative activities for all learners because of the synaesthetic possibilities they offer. Multimodal activities enable seamless movement across languages and modes, facilitating the creation of complex ensembles. This combinatorial activity is an essential ingredient in creative thought (Huizinga, 1950/1955). Bateson and Martin argue that play consists of "actions or . . . thoughts expressed in novel combinations" (2013, p. 12). Creativity is about seeking out and exploring novel approaches and new solutions to issues and problems. It is about using a wide range of media and materials (Beghetto, 2010) but also, I argue, about using a wide range of modes that allow for cognitive flexibility. Because play is not restricted by productivity, it offers different ways of doing things through synaesthetic activity. This "*complementarity* in the *design* of modal ensembles" that ensures when something is " 'missing' in *this* mode here is likely to be available in *that* mode there (Kress, 2015, p. 56) is foundational to creativity. Research that focuses on creativity as synaesthetic activity offers new possibilities for enhancing creative thought and activity in schools but also in workplaces and in higher education.

The underlying premise of these new directions, and what I most want to advocate for in this book, is the recognition that multimodality permeates all aspects of our lives, in all communities, and in all geographic regions. If we fail to recognize this actuality as educators and researchers, we will fail to truly see, understand, and respond to the human condition in all its diversity and complexity.

REFERENCES

Bateson, P., & Martin, P. (2013). *Play, playfulness, creativity, and innovation.* Cambridge: Cambridge University Press.

Beghetto, R. A. (2010). Creativity in the classroom. In J. C. Kaufman, & R. J. Sternberg (Eds.), *The Cambridge handbook of creativity* (pp. 447–466). Cambridge, UK: Cambridge University Press.

Brickman, P., Gormally, C., Armstrong, N., & Hallar, B. (2009). Effects of inquiry-based learning on students' science literacy skills and confidence. *International Journal for the Scholarship of Teaching and Learning, 3*(2). Retrieved from http://www.georgiasouthern.edu/ijsotl

Cazden, C. (1981). Performance before competence: Assistance to child discourse in the zone of proximal development. *Quarterly Newsletter of the Laboratory of Comparative Human Cognition, 3*(1), 5–8.

Dewey, J. (1958). *Experience and nature*. New York, NY: Dover.

Early, M., Kendrick, M., & Potts, D. (2015). Multimodality: Out from the margins of English language teaching. *TESOL Quarterly, 49*(3), 447–460.

Harpaz, Y. (2005). Teaching and learning in a community of thinking. *Journal of Curriculum and Supervision, 20*(2), 136–157.

Harpaz, Y., & Lefstein, A. (2000). Communities of thinking. *Educational Leadership, 58*(3). Retrieved from http://yoramharpaz.com//pubs/en_thinking/cot-in-educational-leadership.pdf

Hmelo-Silver, C., Duncan, R., & Chinn, C. (2007). Scaffolding and achievement in problem-based and inquiry learning: A response to Kirschner, Sweller and Clark (2006). *Educational Psychologist, 42*(2), 99–107. doi: 10.1080/00461520701263368

Huizinga, J. (1950/1955). *Homo Ludens: The study of the play element in culture.* Boston, MA: Beacon Press.

Kress, G. (2015). Applied linguistics and a social semiotic account of multimodality. *AILA Review, 28*, 49–71.

Kuhlthau, C., Maniotes, L., & Caspari, A. (2007). *Guided inquiry: Learning in the 21st century*. Santa Barbara, CA: Greenwood Pub.

McTighe, J., & Wiggins, G. (2013). *Essential questions: Opening doors to student understanding* (2nd ed.). Alexandria, VA: Association for Supervision and Curriculum Development.

Moll, L. C., & Greenberg, J. B. (1990). Creating zones of possibilities: Combining social contexts for instruction. In L. C. Moll (Ed.), *Vygotsky and education: Instructional implications and applications of sociohistorical psychology* (pp. 319–348). New York, NY: Cambridge University Press.

Shanahan, T. (1997). Reading-writing relationships, thematic units, inquiry learning . . . In pursuit of integrated literacy instruction. *Reading Teacher, 51*(1), 12–19.

van Leeuwen, T. (2015). Multimodality in education: Some directions and some questions. *TESOL Quarterly, 49*(3), 582–589.

Wiggins, G., & McTighe, J. (2005). *Understanding by design* (2nd ed.). Alexandria, VA: Association for Supervision and Curriculum Development.

Yamada-Rice, D. (2015). Cultural affordances of visual mode texts in and of Japanese landscapes and young children's emerging comprehension of semiotic texts. In J. Rowsell & K. Pahl (Eds.), *The Routledge handbook of literacy studies* (pp. 308–321). London, UK: Routledge.

Index